5 Steps to Hearing God's Voice

For Those on the Leading Edge of Consciousness

5 Steps to Hearing God's Voice
For Those on the Leading Edge of Consciousness

DavidPaul Doyle

AUTHOR'S EDITION

Published by:
HeartWise Publishing
P.O. Box 3125
Ashland, OR 97520
541-488-0426
www.thevoiceforlove.com

ISBN: 978-1-937621-00-1
Library of Congress Control Number: 2011914643

Cover design by m80branding.com - Wes Youssi

Printed in the United States of America
10   9   8   7   6   5   4   3   2   1

5 Steps to Hearing God's Voice

For Those on the Leading Edge of Consciousness

By DavidPaul Doyle

Also by DavidPaul Doyle

When God Spoke to Me:
The Inspiring Stories Of Ordinary People Who Have
Received Divine Guidance and Wisdom

The Voice for Love:
Hearing Your Inner Voice to
Fulfill Your Life's Purpose
(Written with Candace Doyle)

To my wife, Candace,
without whom this book would not exist

Table of Contents

Introduction   xi

Part One: 5 Steps to Hearing God's Voice   1

Step 1: Extend Love To Your Thoughts   3

Putting the Pieces Together   4

Exercise What Do You Believe?   5

Establishing a Framework   12

Exercise The Barriers to Hearing God's Voice   17

Overcoming the Barriers to Hearing God's Voice   18

Extending Love to Your Thoughts   20

Exercise Step 1: Extend Love to Your Thoughts   26

Being Present With What Is   29

Exercise Step 1: Extend Love to Your Thoughts   31

Extending Love in Your Daily Life   34

Step 2: Feel God's Voice   35

Strengthening Your Awareness   36

Exercise Step 2: Feel God's Voice   39

Step 3: Ask a Question   **45**

    Opening the Door Through Prayer   46

    Crafting Your Question   49

    Exercise Step 3: Ask a Question   51

Step 4: Express God's Voice   **59**

    Hearing a Conversational Voice   60

    The 1st Key to Hearing God's Voice   61

    Exercise Sing to Yourself   63

    Expressing Your True Self   66

    The 2nd Key to Hearing God's Voice   67

    The 3rd Key to Hearing God's Voice   69

    Exercise Express God's Voice using Pen and Paper   71

    How Do You Know?   80

Step 5: Embody God's Voice   **83**

    Step 5: Embody God's Voice   84

    Exercise The 5 Steps to Hearing God's Voice   89

Part Two: Becoming God's Voice in the World   **99**

    Exercise Speak God's Voice Out Loud   100

    Hearing God's Voice in All Ways   111

    Extending Love Without an Egoic Agenda   114

    All Thoughts Serve the Same Purpose   116

    Looking Forward to the Opportunity   117

    The Many Flavors of Love   119

    A Way of Being   119

    Being Present in the Now   120

    Extending Love in Conversation   121

    Exercise Make a Commitment   123

    Exercise Deepening Your Experience of God's Voice   129

Part Three: Being God's Voice in the World   **139**

    Experiencing Your Divine Self   140

      Exercise: Experiencing Your True Self   151

    The Importance of Using God's Voice in the World   155

    All Forms of Hearing Are Equal   156

    Being and Creation   157

    Serving the One that You Are   159

    Being the Voice of God in the World   160

      Exercise Discovering Your Purpose in the World   162

      Exercise Fulfilling Your Purpose in the World   167

      Exercise Staying in Your Right-Mind   168

      Exercise Fulfilling Your Purpose Journal   171

    Your Heart's Desire   179

      Exercise Connecting With Your Heart's Desire   181

    Fulfilling Your Heart's Desire   186

      Exercise Staying in Your Right-Mind   188

      Exercise Fulfilling Your Heart's Desire Journal   190

      Exercise Comparing Your Experiences   198

    Love in Action   202

Introduction

In the summer of 2004 while living in an old barn on the outskirts of Ashland, Oregon, my wife, Candace, and I had just finished writing *The Voice for Love*, our first book on how to hear God's Voice within. Knowing there were no other books like it in print, we confidently submitted it to dozens of publishers expecting it to be an instant success.

"Who wouldn't want to hear God's Voice?" we thought.

To our surprise, the rejection letters came trickling in one by one. Not a single publisher was interested in printing it.

Determined to get our message out any way we could, we published the book ourselves and sent hundreds of review copies to churches and spiritual groups around the country. Several months went by without a word. Then suddenly, the phone began to ring. Ministers and spiritual leaders from all over began inviting us to come teach their parishioners how to hear God's Voice within them. We were thrilled at the response and felt as if our dreams were finally coming true. There was only one problem—we had no idea how to teach them.

That might sound strange since we had just written a book about how to hear God's Voice, but the truth is, we had never taught anyone in person before. The vast majority of *The Voice for Love* was given to us from the Holy Spirit. As a result, writing the book itself was fairly easy. We just asked a lot of questions, recorded the answers we heard within, and then supplemented the messages with our personal experiences.

"How on earth are we going to guide people in actually hearing God's Voice within them after only three or four hours of instruction?" we gasped.

Having no idea what to say or do in a workshop, we did the only thing that made sense—we went within and asked. Just as we did for *The Voice for Love*, we sat down with a digital recorder and started asking Holy Spirit a lot of questions: What conceptual understanding will people need to begin hearing God's Voice? What simple technique can we give them to effectively quiet their minds in just a few minutes? How can we make the experience of hearing God's Voice so undeniably real for them that they'll have no doubt about what they're hearing and can confidently reconnect with this loving Presence within them anytime they want?

Three hours and many questions later, we had it—a simple and direct process for guiding people step-by-step in hearing God's Voice within them as a distinct and conversational voice. We didn't know if it would work, but we were excited to try.

The following week we drove to Eugene, Oregon to give our first workshop. About 20 people attended. Both excited and nervous, we guided everyone through the 5-steps we had been given. To our amazement, each person received specific and clear communication within them by the end of the workshop.

Two weeks later we flew to Cleveland, Ohio, then to Madison, Wisconsin, and finally to Louisville, Kentucky, giving three workshops in ten days. By following the five simple steps we had been given just weeks before, over 100 people experienced hearing God's Voice within them. We were thrilled!

For the next eighteen months, packed to the ceiling in our 1996 Volkswagen Jetta, we crisscrossed the country with our 4-year-old daughter, Hannah, teaching people the 5 Steps. By the time Hannah had started kindergarten, we had conducted over 100 workshops throughout the United States and Canada.

Since then, we have taught tens of thousands of people around the world how to hear God's Voice within them in a very clear and recognizable way using these 5 Steps. Because the steps are so elegantly simple and effective, we are confident that if you practice these steps, you too will hear God's Voice within you, regardless of your background, your faith, or your personal beliefs.

Once you learn these 5 Steps, you will understand why they are guaranteed to work. The key lies in your willingness to practice them. If you truly wish to experience this Divine Presence within you, you must actively participate in this process. Your success in receiving ongoing inner guidance and direction, deepening your experience of the Truth of Who you are, and consciously fulfilling your true purpose in the world rests upon one thing—*practicing* **the exercises in this book.** Our workshops are so successful because people actually *do* the exercises in the workshops. It's *doing* the exercises that gives them the *experience* they are seeking. Learning yet another new concept, theory, or belief will only take you so far, but knowing *what to do* and then **doing it** has the power to change your life.

Reading this book alone will not give you what you want. Reading this book, **practicing the exercises**, and experiencing the results has the power to transform your life. When you come to an exercise, stop reading and *do* the exercise. If you need to practice the exercise for several days before picking up the book again, please do so. You will gain infinitely more by **experiencing** the exercises than by adding yet another spiritual concept or belief to your repertoire. Don't be in a rush to read this entire book at once. Take your time and savor the experience each exercise intends to give you.

The *Author's Edition* of the *5-Steps to Hearing God's Voice* is both a book and a journal. Write in it. Scribble in it. Highlight key sentences and phrases. Answer the questions in the spaces provided, and continue to practice the 5 Steps in the journal section at the end of the book. Your active, written participation inside this book will not only serve as a wonderful account of your personal awakening to hearing God's Voice within you, it will transform your life far more than keeping the book pristine and unmarked on your nightstand or bookshelf.

Thank you for making the decision to hear, share, and *be* the Voice of God in the world. It is a tremendous gift you give to us all.

Many blessings to you.

DavidPaul Doyle
Ashland, Oregon
October 2011

Part One

5 Steps to Hearing God's Voice

Step 1

Extend
Love
To Your
Thoughts

Putting the Pieces Together

Learning to hear God's Voice is a lot like building a jigsaw puzzle. If you have all the pieces and a system for fitting them together, completing the puzzle can be simple, straight-forward, and a lot of fun. It's when pieces are missing and there is no systematic approach for fitting them together that finishing the puzzle can become frustrating to the point that you may feel like giving up.

When I was young, one of our family pastimes was building jigsaw puzzles. The first thing we did when starting a new puzzle was to separate and sort all of the pieces: the four corners, the edges, and all the middle pieces. Once they were separated, we put the four corner pieces into place, completed the border, and then worked our way toward the center.

We will approach learning to hear God's Voice in a similar way, by first identifying and sorting the pieces, building a framework, and then working our way within.

EXERCISE
What Do You Believe?

Your understanding and beliefs about God, your Self, and what it means to hear God's Voice play a significant role in your experience of hearing God's Voice in your life. Whether conscious or subconscious, these thoughts and beliefs impact your experience of feeling worthy enough to hear this Voice. They also impact how you receive divine guidance in your life, what God's Voice sounds like to you, and the types of communication you receive.

Before we put the pieces for hearing God's Voice together, it's important that we first sort through and understand the pieces you already have. Please read the following questions and answer them as thoroughly as you can. Writing your answers down will help you clarify your thoughts and beliefs and will give you the opportunity to refer to them later. Don't worry about answering the questions perfectly. Just write whatever comes to mind. Use these questions as a brainstorming exercise to help you get all of your thoughts and beliefs onto paper. Keep writing until you feel complete.

1. Who or What is God?

_____

_____

_____

_____

_____

_____

_____

_____

_____

_____

_____

_____

_____

_____

_____

_____

_____

_____

_____

_____

_____

_____

_____

_____

_____

_____

_____

2. What is the truth of who I am? What is my true nature and real relationship to God?

_____

_____

_____

_____

_____

_____

_____

_____

_____

_____

_____

_____

_____

_____

_____

_____

_____

_____

_____

_____

_____

_____

3. What is God's Voice? Where is God's Voice?

4. What is the ego?

5. What does it mean to hear God's Voice?

6. Do you believe you are able to hear God's Voice? Why or why not?

_____

_____

_____

_____

_____

_____

_____

_____

_____

_____

_____

_____

_____

_____

_____

_____

_____

_____

_____

_____

_____

_____

_____

Establishing a Framework

I struggled to hear God's Voice for many years. It was an agonizing period in my life. I desperately wanted to receive clear and unmistakable guidance and direction, but no matter what I did or how hard I tried, I just couldn't hear anything. I cried myself to sleep in hopelessness too many times to count.

Looking back on it now, it's easy to see what stopped me. For starters, I unconsciously perceived God and God's Voice as something outside of me. I also harbored the expectation that when I did finally hear God's Voice, it would sound like a big, booming voice in my head. These thoughts and beliefs were so deeply ingrained within me that it never occurred to me to question them. In working with hundreds of people over the years, I have come to learn that we all share these common misperceptions to one degree or another. As a result of our thinking, our experiences of feeling separate from God, coupled with our understanding and expectations about what it means to hear God's Voice, significantly impact our ability to hear this Voice within us in a clear and consistent way.

After years of heartache straining to hear an audible voice in my head with no success, I eventually gave up trying and made peace with hearing God's Voice through signs, intuition, feelings, and in many other ways. Ironically, it was only after I had released all hope of hearing an actual voice within me that one day, quite unexpectedly, I began hearing this Presence of Love as a distinct and clear inner voice.

Several years later when Candace and I sat down to write *The Voice for Love*, we asked the Holy Spirit to describe Who and What this still small Voice within all of us truly is. The answer we received was given to us in the form of a story, and it went something like this:

Before there was time and space, before the earth or anything in the universe existed, there was God.

There are many great words to describe God: Father/Mother, Creator, Pure Spirit, Cosmic Consciousness, Universal Mind, Divine Being, Unconditional Love, All That Is, Source, Infinite Wisdom, Essence of Life, I Am That I Am ... The list could go on and on. For the sake of our description, we'll say that God is Love.

As the story goes, God is simply *being* all that God *is*. Since God *is* Love, God is just extending the Love that God is infinitely, in all directions, and it's this overflowing and extension of God's Love that creates a Child.

This Child of God, this extension of God's Love, is Who We are. We are the extension of God's Infinite Being.

We as the Child of God are simply *being* with God. At One with God and all of existence, we are just being the Infinite Presence of Love that God is, when suddenly, as if out of the blue, a thought bubbles up within the Mind that says, "What would it be like to experience being autonomous? What would it be like to experience being separate from God?"

Now it's not that we could ever *be* separate from God, since we are part of God and God is All That Is, but the thought is, "What *would it be like* to experience being separate from God?"

Being as creative as God is, it's almost as if we scratched our head and thought to our Self, "Hmmm, how could we possibly do that? How could we possibly experience what it's like to be separate from God?"

And then—BANG—it came to us.

What if we could create *a way of thinking* that was so convincing and real that it gave us the opportunity to experience what it *would be like* to be separate from God? What if we could create a way of thinking that helped us to live out this desire to experience being autonomous?

So we did. We created a way of thinking that gives us as the Child of God the opportunity to experience what it's like to be separate from

God, and we'll call this way of thinking the "ego." **That's all the ego is—a way of thinking that gives us the opportunity to experience what it's like to be separate from God, to be separate from Love.**

As God noticed this desire to experience autonomy rise up within the Mind and saw the ego come alive to reinforce that thought, it's as if God said, "No problem. Go off and experience what it would be like to be separate from Love. I am going to create another thought system— one that will always remind you of the Truth of Who You Are, that will always remind you that you *are* Love and remain as I created you to *be*," and God called this new thought system the "Holy Spirit."

To accomplish Its purpose, God extended the Holy Spirit with a dual function. First, the Holy Spirit *knows* the Reality of God. It knows that God *is* All That Is, that only Love is Real, and that we as the Child of God remain exactly as God created us to be. At the same time, the Holy Spirit can perceive *everything* that has ever been made or thought with the ego. It can perceive all of it, but it doesn't believe it.

This double awareness is key. **The Holy Spirit knows that only the Reality of God is True, yet it can perceive everything that has ever been thought with the ego but doesn't believe it.**

We as the Child of God, on the other hand, had to believe in the ego or the experience of separation would never have been real to us in the first place. Believing in the ego was a necessary part of its success. If we never believed its thinking, it would never have been effective in giving us the experience of what it's like to be separate. The Holy Spirit can perceive all that the ego thinks but doesn't believe it and *is* the constant reminder within our Self of the Truth of Who We Are. The Holy Spirit is the part of our own Mind that knows we have never been separate from God and are, in fact, the very Presence of Love that God is.

Of course, it doesn't matter what we call the Holy Spirit. Just like God, there are many great words to describe this Consciousness within all of us: still small Voice, Voice for God, Comforter, Inner Guide,

Inner Teacher, God's Voice, Inner Wisdom, Higher Self, Holy Ghost, Advocate, Voice for Love, our Right-Mind, Unified Consciousness, and many others. Ultimately, it doesn't matter what we call this Divine Voice within. It's seeking it out and connecting with it—by whatever name we choose—that has the power to impact our lives.

So what does it mean then to hear God's Voice?

Very simply, every time we choose the Holy Spirit's thought system instead of the ego's thought system, we are hearing God's Voice. The Holy Spirit is the Voice *for* God, the Voice for God's Reality, the way of thinking that mirrors and reflects God's experience of all. Every time we choose the Holy Spirit's way of thinking instead of the ego's way of thinking, we are hearing God's Voice.

As the Voice for God, the Holy Spirit shares all of the same qualities of God. What are the qualities of God? When we experience Pure Being and our union with God, we experience Joy, Bliss, Love, Happiness, Peace, Acceptance, Generosity, Patience, Understanding, Compassion, Forgiveness, Serenity, Oneness, and many other Love-based emotions. These are the qualities of God—the qualities of Pure Being—and the Holy Spirit shares all of these loved-based qualities as well.

The thought system of the ego, on the other hand, is based upon the qualities of fear, anger, resentment, heartache, loneliness, worry, sadness, frustration, jealousy, and all other separation-based emotions that would drive us to judge and attack one another, be attached to and strive for things in the world, or otherwise cause us to experience being separate from one another and our Source. These are the qualities of the ego.

So what does it mean to hear God's Voice?

Every time we choose a quality of the Holy Spirit, instead of a quality of the ego, we are hearing God's Voice. Every time we choose Peace instead of resentment, Love over fear, Faith instead of worry, or Compassion rather than anger, we are hearing the Voice for God, the

Voice for Peace and Love within each of us that reminds us of the Truth of Who We Are, as well as the Truth of the One in front of us.

You can see from this definition that people all over the world are hearing God's Voice frequently in their lives. We are all hearing God's Voice in so many different ways each and every day, yet we don't often recognize or acknowledge it as such.

As you begin to experience God's Voice more fully and consistently in your life, you will begin to perceive the world through the eyes of Holy Spirit, and all that you once experienced as "less than God" or "less than Love" will simply fall away from your reality.

EXERCISE
The Barriers to
Hearing God's Voice

Before we venture within to begin hearing God's Voice, it's important that we take some time to identify and understand what keeps us from it. Please take a few minutes right now to write down all the things in your life that you think keep you from hearing God's Voice.

_____

_____

_____

_____

_____

_____

_____

_____

_____

_____

_____

_____

_____

_____

_____

_____

_____

_____

Overcoming the Barriers to Hearing God's Voice

The list of barriers that keep people from hearing God's Voice is long indeed. For many, it's a feeling of unworthiness, or the fear of what they might actually hear if God were in fact to speak to them. For others, it may be the judgmental thoughts that fill their minds, or perhaps the belief that they don't have enough time in their busy lives to connect with God. Regardless of what you wrote down in the previous exercise, the barriers to hearing God's Voice all have one thing in common—*they are all just a thought.*

No matter what we perceive as being a barrier to hearing God's Voice, it all boils down to a thought—a thought of unworthiness, a thought of fear or judgment, a thought that we don't have enough time in our lives to join with God. Regardless of what we think is stopping us, it is only "a thought."

We give our thoughts all the meaning they have for us. If a thought of fear arises within our mind, and we give that thought "life" by validating it, judging it, fearing it, suppressing it, or giving it our belief or allegiance, we transform that innocent, meaningless thought into a "real" experience in our reality. In truth, the thought itself has no meaning or power unless we give it meaning or power.

Let me give you an analogy. Imagine that there is just One Mind, and this One Mind is like a river flowing by, stocked full of fish. The fish are the collection of thoughts floating around in this One Mind. A fish goes swimming by in the river and we reach in and pluck it out. We hold the fish up in the air and think to our Self, "Nice fish. How beautiful. I can't wait to eat it. I recently saw a TV show talking about the health benefits of eating fish ... It does kind of smell funny though. I wonder if this is the kind of fish I like ... I read a report once saying fish contain a lot of mercury. Maybe it's not a good idea to eat this fish after all ... I can't believe it. I totally forgot. I'm allergic to fish! I once had an allergy test done and my doctor recommended that I stop eating fish."

If ten people were to reach into the river and pluck out the same fish, each person would experience that fish in a different way because it's the thoughts we think *about the fish* that creates our experience of it, not the fish itself.

Here is another example. Let's say someone wakes up in bed one day and has the thought, "My throat feels sore." Then she thinks, "I feel horrible. This is not good. I hate being sick. I must not be taking good care of myself. I know I brought this sickness on myself. I'm really blowing it. I can't afford to miss work. I know I've done something wrong to bring this sickness on. I'm always doing this to myself. I'm such a failure."

Then another person wakes up and has the same thought, "My throat feels sore." She then thinks, "I feel horrible. What am I going to do? You know what ... I'm going to call in sick today! I've wanted to take a day off work for so long. I really need a break. In fact, I'm going to take two days off, watch a bunch of movies, make myself some chicken soup, and just relax. Maybe I'll catch up on some good reading and write in my journal, too. I can't wait! I've wanted this opportunity to take care of myself for a long time."

Both people have the same exact thought, "My throat feels sore," but it's the way each one relates to that thought that creates their experience, not the thought itself. For one, it is a horrible experience, for the other, a blessing.

Our thoughts have no meaning in and of themselves. Thoughts simply *are.* **We give our thoughts all the meaning they have for us. It is how we relate to our thoughts that creates our experience.** Twenty people could become aware of the same thought within them, and each one will have a different experience depending upon how they relate to that thought.

No matter what you wrote down as a barrier to hearing God's Voice in the previous exercise, *it is only a thought.* It is the meaning, power, validity, and belief that you give to that "thought" that makes it true for you or not. It is how you relate to that thought that impacts your experience, not the thought itself.

As you will soon see in the next section, it is in your relationship to your thoughts where your true power lies.

Extending Love to
Your Thoughts

In this section, I am going to walk you through an exercise for relating to your thoughts in a new way. The first step will be to close your eyes and become aware of everything you notice. **For the purpose of this exercise, we're going to call everything you notice "a thought."** Let me give you a few examples.

When you close your eyes, if you notice the sound of a car driving by, we're going to call that observation "a thought." If you become aware of a sensation in your head, feel your bottom on your chair, or notice your chest rising to take a breath, we're going to call each of those observations "a thought." No matter what you become aware of, we're going to call it "a thought." It could be a sound you hear, a physical sensation or emotion you feel, a person or situation you think about, an image that comes to mind, a concept or belief you notice ... The examples are endless because anything and everything you become aware of when you close your eyes in this next exercise, we're going to call a "thought."

Once you close your eyes and become aware of your "thoughts," your next step will be to practice *relating to those thoughts* exactly the same way the Holy Spirit does. Remember, it's *how we relate to our thoughts* that creates our experience, not the thoughts themselves.

So how does the Holy Spirit relate to thoughts? **The Holy Spirit relates to every thought in exactly the same way. The Holy Spirit perceives every thought and only does one thing— It extends Love.** The Holy Spirit perceives every thought and can only extend *What It Is*. Being the Voice for God's Reality, the Voice for God's Experience, the Holy Spirit can only extend the Love that God *is*. The Holy Spirit is in a "holy relationship" with every thought in existence because it perceives every thought and only extends Love to each one.

There are, of course, many "flavors" of Love, just as there are many qualities of God. The Holy Spirit might extend Compassion, Kindness, Forgiveness, Peace, Grace, Gentleness, Understanding, Patience, Comfort, Gratitude, or any other aspect of Love. All flavors of Love are equal. Regardless of which flavor the Holy Spirit extends to a particular thought, they are all an extension of Love in one form or another.

The way the Voice for Love within us relates to our thoughts is exactly the same way we're going to relate to our own thoughts in this next exercise. We're going to extend Love to every thought we become aware of. What might that look like? Let me give you a few examples.

When you close your eyes in this next exercise to practice extending love to your thoughts, I recommend that you feel your Love going out to every thought you notice. Literally *feel the Love* from your heart extending to whatever enters your awareness. If you are a visual person, you can imagine golden or white light flowing to your thoughts and surrounding them. If you are kinesthetic, you might imagine physically embracing your thoughts, wrapping your arms around them or rocking them back and forth like a baby. If you are auditory, you may prefer to thank your thoughts or bless each one, literally saying the words, "Thank you," or "Bless you," silently within yourself.

These are just a few examples of the many ways we can "extend Love to our thoughts." Each of these examples is an "expression of Love." It doesn't matter what form your Love takes or how it is expressed. There are no right ways to extend Love. You can choose any one of these methods, combine them together, or create your own. What's important is that you "extend Love to your thoughts" in one form or another. The flavor or expression of Love you choose is irrelevant. It's the intention and sincerity behind the expression that matters.

If you are uncertain what "extending Love" looks like for you, or need a little help connecting with the love within you, close your eyes and ask yourself, "What do I love unconditionally?"

I once directed a group of people to ask themselves this question. One gentleman closed his eyes for a few moments and said, "My dog. I love my dog."

I replied, "Perfect. Imagine your dog running into the room right now. How do you react to your dog running into the room?"

With his eyes still closed, the man threw open his arms and called out, "Come here boy! Come here!"

I said, "That! Right there! That's extending Love. I want you to do that with every thought you become aware of in this next exercise."

One woman who loves trees saw herself going up to a tree and giving it a big hug. Another woman who loves babies imagined holding a baby in her arms and rocking it. Once you discover how you naturally express Love, extend that Love in exactly the same way to every thought you become aware of in this next exercise.

If you have difficulty finding an expression of Love that works for you, experiment with different ways of extending Love until you find a good fit. You may discover that it comes to you when you least expect it. For example, you might start the exercise by thanking every thought, but as your gratitude builds, you may realize that you're no longer saying the words "Thank you" but instead simply *feeling* your gratitude naturally extending to everything you notice. Or maybe you visualize sending golden light to your thoughts, but after a few minutes find yourself thinking the words "Bless you" as you surround every thought in golden light.

What's important is the intention and sincerity behind the Love you extend, not the form or expression the Love takes. For most people, *feeling* their Love radiating to their thoughts intensifies the experience, so if you're able to feel the emotion you're extending— whether it's Love, Gratitude, Compassion, or any other flavor of Love—please do so. If you're not able to feel the expression of Love you're extending in that moment, that's okay. Your experience of extending Love will continue to evolve and deepen the longer you practice this process.

Before we begin the exercise, I'd like to address a few things. First, noticing our thoughts can sometimes be a little tricky. When we're not in the habit of recognizing everything in our awareness as "a thought," our thoughts can sometimes be so subtle that we aren't even aware we're thinking them, such as noticing that we're sitting in a room, feeling different sensations in our body, or even having the thought, "I'm not aware of having any thoughts right now." Remember, ANYTHING and EVERYTHING we become aware of in this exercise is a "thought" in one form or another. EVERYTHING.

In addition, there will be times when your thoughts all seem to come at once. For example, let's say you're sitting there with your eyes closed and you suddenly think of your mother who was recently in a car accident. You see a picture of her smashed-up car in your mind. You see her sitting on her couch in pain with no one to take care of her. You notice a sharp burning sensation in your chest. You feel angry at the person who rear-ended her car, sad she's in so much pain, guilty for not spending more time with her, enraged at the insurance company for not paying her claim, and ashamed for yelling at your children on the way to school that morning.

Dozens of interrelated thoughts and feelings may surge through your awareness all at once. They may come so quickly you can't even identify them all. When the thoughts finally stop, you may be left experiencing an amalgamation of them all or perhaps just the last thought that went through your mind.

If you become aware of a sudden burst of thoughts like this when you practice the following exercise, don't worry about identifying each individual thought. Just pick one thought out of the crowd and extend Love to it. Whether it's the rage you feel toward the insurance company, the thought of your mother in pain, the pressure you feel in your chest, or the guilt you feel for yelling at your children, just pick one of those thoughts and extend Love to it. It doesn't matter which thought you choose. **Every thought serves the same purpose. Every thought gives you the opportunity to extend Love.**

Inevitably a thought will eventually surface in your awareness that you won't want to extend Love to. It could be a person you dislike, a traumatic event in your life, or an intense feeling of sadness, anger, or fear. When you become aware of not wanting to extend Love to a particular thought, remind yourself that it is literally *just a thought*. The moment before, you were not even aware of that person, situation, or emotion. Then a thought arose about that person or situation and you instantly felt sad or upset. The person is not literally standing in front of you. The situation is not actually unfolding before your eyes. They are *just thoughts* within your mind. You are not being asked to send Love to the person or situation. You are simply being asked to extend Love *to the thought* of the person or situation. It may be helpful to remember this when you resist extending Love to a thought that surfaces in your awareness.

If you're not able to extend Love to a particular thought, that's okay. Extend Love to whatever thoughts you can, or extend Love to the thought that you don't want to extend Love to that thought. Remember, it doesn't ultimately matter which thoughts you choose to extend Love to. Just extend Love to whatever thoughts you can in that moment.

Finally, it's important to make a distinction between "loving your thoughts" and "extending Love to your thoughts." To the ego, loving your thoughts means you like them, want them, think they're good thoughts, or agree with them and want to hold onto them. That's the ego's definition of love, and that's not what we're talking about. We're talking about extending Love *to your thoughts*.

Let's take a look at how the ego relates to thought. When a thought passes through our mind, the ego immediately judges that thought. The ego judges every thought that goes through our mind: We either like it or we don't like it. We think it's a good thought or a bad thought, a spiritual thought or a not-so-spiritual thought. We want to hold onto it or get rid of it. We believe it or we don't believe it. The ego is always judging. It is always determining what to do to a thought or with a thought. And if it's not immediately choosing to like it or dislike it, keep it or get rid of it, it's choosing to improve upon it, upgrade it, or make it better. This is the way the ego relates to thought, and it's always from a place of judgment, no matter how subtle that judgment may be.

The Holy Spirit, on the other hand, doesn't *do* any of that. **The Holy Spirit extends Love to every thought in existence, indiscriminately and unconditionally. It is in a holy, unconditionally loving relationship with all of creation. It does not discern but only loves. It perceives everything and can only extend What It is, which is Love.**

This is exactly how we're going to relate to our own thoughts in the next exercise. We are going to extend Love to every thought that enters our awareness.

EXERCISE
Step 1: Extend Love to Your Thoughts

1. Find a comfortable place to sit and close your eyes.
2. Notice that whatever you become aware of is "a thought" and extend Love to that thought in whatever form or expression feels natural to you.
3. Continue to extend Love to your thoughts for at least five minutes. There's no need to rush or to extend Love to every thought as quickly as you can. Take your time and enjoy the process.
4. When you're done, take a few minutes to answer the following questions.

DESCRIBE YOUR EXPERIENCE

1. What happened to your thoughts when you extended Love to them? Did your thoughts start to slow down or become fewer in number the longer you extended Love? Please describe.

_____

_____

_____

_____

_____

_____

2. What was your overall experience of extending Love? What did you feel or experience as a result? Please describe.

Being Present
With What Is

What most people discover when they extend Love to their thoughts is that their thoughts suddenly disappear. Similar to the idea that darkness cannot exist in the presence of Light, or fear cannot exist in the presence of Love, when we extend Love to our thoughts, our thoughts simply fall away. What we are left with is Peace, Love, Joy, Compassion, or one of the many other qualities of God. **When we extend Love, giving and receiving become one. By extending Love, we receive it. By giving our blessings, we become blessed.**

If you didn't notice that your thoughts started to slow down and fall away as you extended Love to them, or you found yourself struggling with this exercise, don't give up or feel discouraged. For most of us, this is an entirely new way of relating to our thoughts. We are habituated to the ego's way of thinking. We are used to relating to our thoughts, our self, and the world with the ego. It can take a little time and practice to adjust to this new way of being in relationship.

In addition, you may have noticed that some thoughts tend to disappear more quickly than others. Because we give our thoughts all the meaning they have for us, if we extend Love to a highly charged thought, emotion, or belief, it will likely take a little longer to dissolve than one that has little or no meaning for us.

Imagine that a thought is like a balloon. Unless we fill the balloon with life, in this case with our breath, the balloon contains no energy or power. When we experience a painful thought, it's because we've imbued that thought with the life energy of the ego. We've infused that thought with judgment, fear, survival, pain, need, desire, attachment, belief, or possibly our own sense of identity. When we give a thought that much "life," it can feel as if we're holding a thousand full helium balloons all tied together, not just a single empty balloon. This is why we oftentimes find ourselves instantly carried away by a painful thought when it arises within us. We immediately feel ungrounded, disconnected, and out of control.

The only difference between a thought that is difficult to let go of and one that is easy to release is the amount of life force you've given to it. When you find yourself face-to-face with an intense or painful thought, regardless of the form it takes (i.e. emotion, belief, sensation, etc.), endeavor to remind yourself that you are *not* the thought itself. **You are the one *experiencing* the thought.**

When you experience a highly charged thought or emotion, it's as if the life energy you've given to that thought pulls your awareness right into it and the thought quickly becomes your entire reality. When you're able to remember that what you're experiencing is only "a thought" that you've given a lot of power and energy to, you empower yourself to pull your awareness out of that thought and see it for what it truly is—**an opportunity to extend Love.** Once you make this shift in your relationship to that thought, the process of disempowering or deflating that thought has already begun.

In these moments, allow yourself to remain present with your experience. Instead of suppressing the painful thought, emotion, belief, or sensation, allow yourself to *be* with it. This will keep the thought at the forefront of your conscious mind and give you the opportunity to extend Love, Compassion, Understanding, or Blessings to it, just as you would to a friend or child in need. Every moment that you join with a painful thought in this way, you drain the life force from that thought. Eventually, there will be no energy or power left within it, and it will quietly dissolve into the very Presence of Love that God is.

EXERCISE
Step 1: Extend Love to Your Thoughts

Before we learn the next step in this 5-step process, I'd like you to practice extending Love to your thoughts one more time. **Step 1: Extend Love to Your Thoughts** is the foundation we're going to build upon for the remainder of these exercises, so it's important to be able to use this step as a means for quieting your mind. If you don't find that your thoughts slow down or fall away as you practice this step, be patient, gentle, and compassionate with yourself. Remember, it's the intention and sincerity behind the love you extend that matters, not the form or expression it takes. As your understanding and practice of "extending Love" deepens, you will have the solid foundation you need to be able to join with and hear this Voice for Love within you under any and all circumstances in your life.

1. Find a comfortable place to sit and close your eyes.
2. Notice that whatever you become aware of is "a thought" and then extend Love to that thought in whatever form or expression feels comfortable to you.
3. Continue to extend Love to your thoughts **for at least seven minutes.** There's no need to rush or extend Love to every thought as quickly as possible. Take your time and enjoy the process.
4. When you're done, take a few minutes to answer the following questions.

DESCRIBE YOUR EXPERIENCE

1. What happened to your thoughts when you extended Love to them? Did your thoughts start to slow down or become fewer in number the longer you extended Love? Please describe.

_____

_____

_____

_____

_____

_____

_____

_____

_____

_____

_____

_____

_____

_____

_____

_____

_____

_____

_____

2. What was your overall experience of extending Love? What did you feel or experience as a result? Please describe.

Extending Love in Your Daily Life

Extending Love to our thoughts can happen anytime, anywhere. While it's wonderful to practice with our eyes closed as a way to access that quiet place within us, extending Love to our thoughts while we're out in the world with our eyes open has the power to bring us a deep experience of peace, love, and connection in all that we do.

Because everything is a thought in one form or another, we can extend Love to every thought that exists. Whether it seems to exist within our own mind or "out in the world," it doesn't matter. The experience of extending Love remains the same. As you set this book down and go about your day, practice extending Love to whatever arises in your life. You might extend Love to the cars as you're driving down the freeway, to everyone sitting around the table in your next business meeting, to the pain you feel in your lower back, or to the frustration you might feel when your friend hasn't called you like he or she promised. Practice extending Love in your daily life and see what happens when you do.

Step 2

Feel God's Voice

Strengthening
Your Awareness

Once we've extended Love to our thoughts in Step 1, and our thoughts have slowed down and fallen away and we find ourselves left in that quiet place within where God's Voice is, the next step is to strengthen our awareness of that Voice.

In Truth, we can't strengthen our connection to God's Voice. We already have this Voice in our lives. It is part of us. God's Voice is integrated into the very fabric of our *Being*. Our connection to God's Voice simply *is*. It cannot be strengthened. Our connection to God's Voice is as strong now as it's always been and will ever be. The only thing we can do is strengthen *our experience* of it. **We are One with God and God's Voice. We can't be any closer, and our connection can't be any stronger. The only thing that might be lacking is our awareness of it**, and that's what we're going to strengthen in *Step 2: Feel God's Voice*.

As a sentient being, your ability to *feel* impacts your experience physically, emotionally, and mentally, which is why feeling is such an important step in this overall process. Once you've spent some time with *Step 1: Extend Love to Your Thoughts* and you find yourself in that quiet place within, transition to *Step 2: Feel God's Voice* and begin to consciously *feel* God's Voice within you. Allow yourself to feel this Divine Presence emotionally, physically, and with every fiber of your being. Take slow, deep breaths and begin to feel God's Voice within you, deeper and deeper with every breath you take.

If you don't know what God's Voice feels like to you, or you feel uncertain how to go about feeling this Presence within you, begin by thinking of something in your life that you are grateful for. It doesn't matter what it is. Just think of anything you are truly grateful for in your life. Once you know what it is, allow yourself to feel your gratitude for it more and more fully with every breath you take. Allow the gratitude you feel to build and grow within you, until eventually you're overflowing with gratitude. For some, this may be a passive process, as if you're surrendering to the gratitude you feel within. For others, you may need to take a more active role in purposely feeling deeper and deeper into your gratitude. Either way, this building of gratitude may take several minutes to unfold, so please be patient. Your only goal is to feel as much gratitude as you possibly can. Take as long as you need to do that.

Once you find yourself filled with gratitude, I want you to then ask God's Voice within you what It feels like. You can ask this question silently or out loud. You might say, "Holy Spirit, what do you feel like?" or "God's Voice, what do you feel like?" Feel your desire to know what the Voice of God within you feels like, then ask your question directly with the sincere intention to receive an answer.

Regardless of the words you use or how you phrase your question, notice what comes into your awareness immediately after you ask your question. You might feel an emotion such as peace, joy, or comfort. You might sense a warmth, pressure, tingling sensation, or presence around your chest, head, or body. You might notice thoughts come into your awareness, such as, "I am the gratitude and love you are feeling." What you notice or become aware of right after you ask your question may be strong and powerful, or it may be so subtle it's barely perceptible. Regardless of the form your answer takes, SOMETHING will come to you. When it does, grab onto it. Whatever answer, feeling, thought, picture, sensation, or knowingness comes to you, grab onto it and feel that answer with everything you've got. Feel deeper and deeper into it, and let that feeling fill your Being. Let it become your entire awareness. This is the purpose of Step 2—to simply feel this Voice of God within you as deeply and fully as you can—by whatever name you call it.

Before we practice Steps 1 and 2 together for the first time, I'd like to address two points. First, visualization can often play a helpful role in deepening your experience of feeling God's Voice in Step 2. Actively visualizing the Presence of Holy Spirit/God's Voice within you while you are feeling deeper and deeper into it can help to amplify your experience of it.

For myself, I often visualize Holy Spirit as an infinite expanse of Golden Light that is shining through and part of everything—everything I imagine to be "within me" and everything I imagine to be "outside of me." Sometimes, I feel into this all-encompassing expanse of Golden Light and allow myself to experience what it feels like. Other times, I ask Holy Spirit what it feels like and then incorporate this Golden Light visualization into the answer I receive.

You do not have to include visualization as part of Step 2. Visualization is simply another form of perception that can be used to help strengthen our awareness of God's Voice. If you do choose to include it, feel free to do so however you like. There is truly no right or wrong way to incorporate visualization in this process.

Finally, if you find it difficult to feel God's Voice in Step 2, continue to ask Holy Spirit what it feels like and notice what comes into your awareness when you do. The Holy Spirit is within all of creation, so whatever comes into your awareness after sincerely asking your question, just feel into it and you will feel the Holy Spirit's Presence within it.

If you find it difficult to feel anything at all in Step 2, don't give up. Be patient with yourself and keep putting one foot in front of the other. As you continue to join with Holy Spirit in different ways throughout this 5-Step Process, you will begin to create a safer, more trusting relationship with your thoughts and feelings. This will eventually give you the courage, willingness, and ability to feel the Holy Spirit in a way that is nurturing and healing for you. In time, your experience of feeling God's Voice will naturally unfold.

EXERCISE
Step 2: Feel God's Voice

1. **Step 1: Extend Love to Your Thoughts** until you find yourself in that quiet place within.
2. **Step 2: Feel God's Voice** within you.
3. If you are uncertain what God's Voice feels like to you, think of something you are grateful for in your life. Let your gratitude for it build within you until you are overflowing with gratitude.
4. Ask God's Voice what it feels like.
5. Grab onto whatever answer comes to mind and feel it as deeply and fully as you can.
6. Allow the feeling of God's Voice to fill your entire awareness.
7. When you feel complete, open your eyes and take a few minutes to answer the following questions.

DESCRIBE YOUR EXPERIENCE

1. What was your experience of extending Love to your thoughts? Please describe.

_____

_____

_____

_____

_____

_____

_____

_____

2. **What thought or answer came to you when you asked God's Voice what it feels like? Please describe.**

3. Describe your experience of feeling God's Voice.

4. Have you felt this experience or feeling before? If so, when?

Step 3

Ask a
Question

Opening the Door Through Prayer

Extending Love to our thoughts gently guides us into the quiet place within so we can more clearly hear God's Voice. Actively feeling this Presence helps us to strengthen our mental, emotional, and physical experience of it. Once we consciously experience this Voice more fully, the next step is to begin the conversation.

Prayer can be thought of as any communication directed to God. It doesn't matter what we pray for or how we pray, the simple act of talking *to God* opens the door to a dialogue *with God*.

Prayer is necessary when we do not fully experience our union with God. If we fully knew our Oneness with God, the Holy Spirit's function would be complete and prayer would serve no purpose. We would be wholly joined with God in our awareness and we would naturally and without question *experience being* the Presence of Love that God *is*. Prayer is the acknowledgment that we are experiencing separation in one form or another and wish to re-connect with God in our experience. So if we want to receive guidance, understanding, or communication from God, it's important for us to begin the conversation with God ... through the Holy Spirit.

Why do *we* have to begin the conversation?

To answer this question, let's take a look at prayer from the Holy Spirit's perspective. God *is* Pure Love. As an extension of God, Pure Love is what we *are* as well. It's our Essence and True Nature. It's what makes up the very fabric of our *Being*. Because the Holy Spirit sees past all form and appearance to the Truth of Who We Are, the Holy Spirit sees only our Wholeness, our Oneness, and our Perfection.

The Holy Spirit does not see us through the eyes of the ego and therefore does not believe we are the bodies we appear to be in the world. It sees only through the eyes of Love and knows that our True

Identity *is* the eternal Spirit and Essence within, surrounding, and sourcing all things. Regardless of what seems to rise and pass away, the Holy Spirit knows that we remain as God created us to be.

By only recognizing our True Nature—that we *are* the Life-Force *within all things*, and not the things themselves—the Holy Spirit knows that we lack nothing. From the Holy Spirit's perspective, **unless we specifically ask for something**, what is there to give us? There is nothing to give us from the Holy Spirit's perspective because It sees only our Perfect Union with God at all times. What could the Holy Spirit give us that we don't already have when we *are* "All That Is" along with God?

So why is it necessary for us to begin the conversation with God? Because *we are the ones* who perceive having wants, needs, trauma, confusion, judgment, fear, and challenges in our lives. We are the ones who identify with and believe the thought system of the ego. **When we are in our Right-Mind—the part of our Mind that shares the Holy Spirit's awareness**—we do not experience the painful delusions of the ego because we are only thinking with the Holy Spirit. We are only thinking with the Voice for God's Reality. It is only when we are out of our Right-Mind, experiencing and believing the pain and struggle of the ego's way of thinking, that prayer becomes necessary for us.

If we experience a want or need within us—whether it's a desire to feel God's Love, receive clear guidance or communication, or to understand why things seem to be unfolding in a particular way—when we bring these wants and needs *to God*, the Holy Spirit instantly joins us exactly where we are and gives us the communication, comfort, and understanding that we seek.

If we do not seek these things in our lives, why would the Holy Spirit presume we need answers or solutions to them? The Holy Spirit is not sitting on high looking down upon the world and thinking, "Look at that guy. He's in serious trouble. He has no idea what he's doing. He's really making a big mistake. I had better go do something about that," or "That lady looks confused. I'll go tell her what to think so she does the right thing."

Remember, the Holy Spirit sees only our Perfection and Wholeness because It only recognizes the Truth of Who We Are, not what the ego would lead us to believe about ourselves. So if we don't seek communication or guidance in our lives, we will not receive it ... but the instant we do seek it, it will be given to us. **The Holy Spirit will deny us nothing, but we must first ask in order for it to be given.**

It is important to acknowledge that prayer can happen on many different levels. Prayer is any communication directed to God. It can be a single thought or feeling, an intention, a long drawn-out monologue, or even an unconscious desire within our heart and mind. Any communication—on any level of Being—that is directed to Source is considered prayer ... and God answers all prayers, through the Holy Spirit.

Imagine for a moment that the Consciousness of the Holy Spirit is integrated into the very fabric of all Creation and Being. This Divine Consciousness is literally part of us, and part of everything that exists. As a result, everything that we truly seek in our hearts, including love, truth, wisdom, inspiration, divine guidance, forgiveness, right-mindedness, grace, healing, abundance, and all other qualities of God, is ever present. Everything we long for in our lives is all around us and within us in every moment, always available to us wherever we are. It is only when we identify with and believe the thoughts of the ego that we do not consciously experience having or receiving these qualities of God in our lives. So it is through our prayers, desires, passions, and intentions that we release our hold on the ego's way of thinking and join our conscious awareness with that of the Holy Spirit's. The instant we do, we receive what has truly been there for us all along.

So if we want something in life, it's up to us to ask for it. It's up to us to put it out there and do whatever it takes within ourselves, and in the world, to receive it. God answers all prayers instantly, but how and when we receive what it is we are asking for is up to us. Luckily, we can turn to this Inner Guide and Comforter to help us take each step along the way with as much support, guidance, and faith as we are willing and able to receive.

Crafting Your Question

Because the Holy Spirit sees only our Perfection and is not capable of judging us in any way, It joins with us exactly "where we are" in communicating to us and answering our questions. As a result, the intentions we hold and the questions we ask play a significant role in what we receive.

As an example, let's take a look at the following questions: Should I turn left or right? Is it in my highest good to turn left or right? Which would be a better path to take, left or right? What would I learn if I went left versus right? What are the pros and cons of going right versus left? What would be the most fulfilling path to take, left or right? Which way would be filled with the most grace and ease, right or left? God, do you want me to go left or right? God, can you tell me which way to go, right or left? Which direction, left or right, will deepen my union with You more fully? With what intention should I go left or right? Does it matter whether I go left or right? What would be in my highest good to keep in mind as I think about going left or right? Are there other options besides going left or right? The list of variations could go on and on.

Because each one of these questions includes a unique intention, bias, and/or assumption, the communication and insight you receive in response to each question will also be unique. Each answer will be filled with Truth, but what is shared and how it is presented to you will be different depending upon the questions you ask. Your deepest intentions will yield the kind of answers you are ready to receive at this time.

In addition, the more sincerity you bring to your questions, the more you'll receive from the answers. For example, if you ask a question that you really don't care about, the answer will not likely impact you very deeply. If you ask a question that has real meaning and significance for you, and you are sincere in wanting an answer, the answer you receive will have a much greater impact upon you. With practice you will develop greater clarity and skill in formulating your questions for the most rewarding outcome.

Step 3: Ask a Question

It is now time to ask God a question and receive an answer. As before, find a comfortable place to sit, close your eyes, and start with *Step 1: Extend Love to Your Thoughts*. Depending upon your state of mind, you may need to extend Love to your thoughts for two minutes, five minutes, or longer until your thoughts slow down and you find yourself in that quiet place within.

When you're ready, transition to *Step 2: Feel God's Voice*. If you're uncertain how to feel God's Voice, or you prefer to begin with gratitude as a bridge to feeling God's Voice, find something in your life that you're grateful for and then feel deeper and deeper into your gratitude until it feels as if it's overflowing within you. Once you are filled with gratitude, ask God's Voice within you what it feels like and allow yourself to receive an answer in any form it is given. Whether the answer is a feeling, thought, sensation, knowingness, picture, still small voice whispering within you, or something entirely different, allow yourself to receive the answer and then feel into that answer as deeply and fully as you can. Allow the feeling of God's Voice to fill your entire awareness.

Once you've experienced Steps 1 and 2, it's time for *Step 3: Ask a Question*. You can ask anything you want on any topic. It can be a question you've previously pondered, or it can be whatever is in your heart and mind in that moment. It can be a specific question about something in your life, or it can be a general question such as, "Do you have anything you would like to tell me right now?" or "What would be in my highest good to hear in this moment?" Once you have asked your question, it is time to be quiet and listen for the reply.

In this particular exercise, be open to receiving the answer in any form it might be given. Do not try to hear specific words within you. We will work on hearing specific words from God's Voice in an upcoming exercise. **For the purpose of this exercise, it's important to be open to hearing God's Voice *in all ways*.** For example, you may feel the answer emotionally or as a physical or energetic sensation. You might see a picture or vision in your mind's eye or experience a shift in perception, understanding, or perspective. You may notice thoughts coming to mind or have an immediate sense of knowing or intuition. In this particular exercise, simply be open to receiving the communication however it comes to you. Don't limit the possibilities by specifically expecting or trying to hear a voice talking to you in words.

Finally, if you notice any thoughts of fear, unworthiness, or doubt come to mind at any time, extend Love to those thoughts, and to any other thoughts that you need to in order to keep yourself connected and in your Right-Mind throughout the process.

1. **Step 1: Extend Love to Your Thoughts** until you find yourself in that quiet place within.

2. **Step 2: Feel God's Voice** within you. Feel it directly, or use gratitude as a bridge.

3. **Step 3: Ask a Question.** You can ask Holy Spirit a specific question or a general question. You can ask the question out loud or silently within yourself, whichever you prefer.

4. Be still and notice what comes into your awareness. Allow yourself to become aware of the answer in any form it is given to you.

5. When you feel complete, open your eyes and answer the following questions as thoroughly as you can. Writing your experience down on paper is important because it will help you to validate and re-affirm your experience.

DESCRIBE YOUR EXPERIENCE

1. What was your experience of extending Love to your thoughts? Please describe.

_____

_____

_____

_____

_____

_____

_____

_____

_____

_____

_____

_____

_____

_____

_____

_____

_____

_____

_____

2. What did God's Voice feel like?

_____

_____

_____

_____

_____

_____

_____

_____

_____

3. What was the exact question you asked?

_____

_____

_____

_____

_____

_____

_____

_____

_____

4. Did you receive an answer in one form or another? If so, what was the answer and in what form did you receive it? Describe your experience. If you did not consciously receive an answer, describe your experience. Did you remember to extend Love to whatever thoughts and emotions might have arisen in the process?

5. **How has your experience shifted or changed as a result of receiving an answer or going through this process? Please describe.**

Step 4

Express God's Voice

Hearing a Conversational Voice

For many years, Candace and I would sit up in bed each Sunday morning and join with God. I would ask a lot of questions, and she would share messages from Holy Spirit. One morning while she was delivering a message, the Holy Spirit speaking through her told me to open my mouth and start speaking this Voice aloud as Candace was. At that time in my life, I had given up trying to hear God's Voice as a distinct and audible voice within me and had made peace with hearing God's Voice in other ways, including signs, feelings, books, movies, and through other people. Candace had been sharing Holy Spirit's voice with me for five years and had never spoken those words before. Surprised at what had been said and a bit nervous to try yet again after so many failed attempts, I silently agreed, opened my mouth, and began speaking God's Voice out loud for the first time. The intense love, certainty, and energy I felt was so deeply moving that I cried tears of joy for quite some time afterwards.

I had always imagined that hearing God's Voice would be like hearing an audible voice in my head, as if I were talking to someone on the telephone. I thought I would hear discernible words spoken to me within my mind and then repeat those words out loud for others to hear. On this special occasion, I didn't hear anything within me at all—not a single word. **I heard the words for the very first time myself as I spoke them out loud to Candace.**

Looking back on my own experience of learning to hear God's Voice and in working with thousands of people on how to open up to hearing this Voice within them, I have identified three common misperceptions that keep most people from hearing God's Voice as clearly and specifically as they would like.

Through a greater understanding of what the Holy Spirit is and how this part of our Self works with us and through us in the world, we can transform these common misunderstandings into the very keys that empower us to hear God's Voice in a clear and recognizable way. The ease and conistency with which we hear God's Voice rests upon these three keys.

The 1ˢᵗ Key to Hearing God's Voice

As shared in Chapter 1 on page 14, "The Holy Spirit is the part of our own mind that knows we have never been separate from God and are, in fact, the very Presence of Love that God is."

The Holy Spirit, by whatever name we call it, is the part of our Self that knows the Truth of Who We Are. It is the part of our mind that knows that our True Identity is eternal, formless, changeless, and beyond any *thing* we might perceive ourselves to be in the world.

The 1ˢᵗ key to hearing God's Voice is that the Holy Spirit is not outside of you. It is not a separate Being or Entity. It is the part of YOU that shares the awareness of God. It is the part of you that is happy, at peace, trusts all things, allows all things, and knows that you remain as you were created to be.

Because we are identified with the ego's way of thinking, we unconsciously perceive the Holy Spirit to be outside of us, greater than us, or somehow *other* than who we are. We think we're seeking guidance or communication from some grander, wiser, separate Being in heaven who somehow stands apart from our own mind or soul. The truth is, God's Voice is part of us. It is the part of our mind, the part of our Self, the part of our awareness, that sees all things through the eyes of Love.

No matter how subtle our experience of separation may be, we are constantly projecting this separation onto God and the Holy Spirit because that is what the ego does—it projects separation. That is the ego's purpose and function, and it does its job perfectly, just as we designed it. So it's not wrong or bad that we perceive God and the Holy Spirit as separate from us. It's just important to be aware that the thoughts and beliefs that promote that way of thinking can only come from the ego because God and Holy Spirit only know our Oneness.

The 1st key to hearing God's Voice is the recognition that God's Voice is not outside of you, but is in fact the part of your own mind that knows the Reality of God. **It's the part of your Self, called by many different names, that knows only Love, shares only Love, and speaks to you only of Love, for that is What It Is and Who You Are.**

How does this 1st key impact you in hearing specific words from God's Voice within you?

To answer this question, let's take a look at how we create words in the world. What are some of the different ways that we might manifest words? We might speak them out loud using our mouth, tongue, and vocal cords. We might pick up a pen and write words on a piece of paper. We might type them on a computer, paint them on a wall, or even use our hands to form words in sign language. In all of these examples, we are using the body as a means to express or manifest words in the world.

Because God's Voice is part of our mind and is not a separate Being or Entity from us, the Holy Spirit uses the body in exactly the same ways to express words to us and others.

EXERCISE
Sing to Yourself

Before we take this idea a step further, please take a few minutes to do the following exercise:

1. Close your eyes and extend Love to your thoughts.

2. Once your thoughts have slowed down, sing the alphabet or another song that you know well silently within yourself for about one minute. Although you aren't singing out loud or making any audible noise with your mouth, sing joyfully and passionately within yourself as if you're filling the room with your song.

3. As you silently sing to yourself, notice HOW you are forming the words. Do you notice that your tongue or vocal cords are ever so slightly moving or vibrating to help form the words, or are you forming the words using only your mind, completely detached, separate, and free from your body altogether? Take as much time as you need to experience HOW the words are being formed when you sing joyfully within yourself.

4. When you are done, answer the following questions.

DESCRIBE YOUR EXPERIENCE

1. Who was forming the words in your song?

_____

_____

_____

_____

2. What was forming the words in your song?

3. How were the words being formed in your song?

_____

_____

_____

_____

_____

_____

_____

_____

_____

_____

_____

_____

_____

_____

_____

_____

_____

_____

_____

_____

_____

_____

Expressing Your True Self

Over the years, I've walked thousands of people through this exercise. Roughly half of the people have reported using their tongues, lips, and/ or vocal cords to one degree or another in order to form words and sentences within their awareness, while the other half have reported experiencing no connection at all with their bodies when forming words and sentences within them.

When I first spoke God's Voice out loud that memorable morning with Candace, I still perceived the Holy Spirit as separate from myself and didn't understand how the Holy Spirit uses the body to communicate to us and through us in the world. After my first few weeks of speaking God's Voice, I felt a little confused because I still wasn't hearing audible words in my head. I kept thinking that speaking the words out loud would somehow open me up to hearing God's Voice audibly within my mind, but it never happened. One day, I asked God why I was still not hearing Its Voice as an actual voice in my head and why I still had to speak the words out loud in order to hear them myself. The answer I received changed my life.

I was told that for the point I had reached on my spiritual path, hearing a seemingly separate voice in my head would create more of an experience of separation from God than union. Hearing an integrated voice, one that was part of me and not separate from my own voice, would serve me better in deepening my experience of union with God. Deep within my heart, hearing a separate voice was not what I wanted, so I was not giving that experience to myself. Hearing God's Voice as my own True Voice was the experience I most desired and thus the reason I was hearing and sharing God's Voice in that way.

This communication from Holy Spirit, which I received by speaking out loud, had a profound impact on me. It erased my belief that I needed to hear a loud voice in my head in order to receive clear and specific communication from God. It also erased my desire to hear God's Voice as an audible voice within me because I knew that the way I was hearing God's Voice was perfect for my own learning and growth. I finally understood *experientially* that God and God's Voice were not outside of me. They were part of me, and I was part of them. I wasn't "channeling" something separate from me. **I was joining with the part of my own Consciousness that *is* God's Voice and expressing that Consciousness in the form of words to myself and others through my body.**

To this day when I go within to hear God's Voice in a conversational manner, I do not hear a single word within me unless I engage my body in some way. By needing to use my body in one form or another to hear and share God's Voice, I've come to realize the gift that it is for me in deepening my experience of union with God and Holy Spirit.

This is the 1st key to hearing God's Voice—acknowledging and embracing your union with God's Voice. Holy Spirit is not a separate being or entity. It is the part of You—the part of your own Mind and Consciousness—that sees the world through God's eyes. Holy Spirit is not separate from you in any way. It is your own Voice you listen to as It speaks to you. It is your own Words It speaks. You are simply joining with the part of your Self that knows only Love and expressing that part of your Self using your body as a communication device.

The 2nd Key to Hearing God's Voice

The 2nd key to hearing God's Voice is the idea that Holy Spirit speaks to us "where we are" on our path of learning and growth.

Let me give you an example. Pretend there is a row of seven people sitting in front of you: a 6-year-old child, a physicist, a Catholic priest, a rebellious teenager, a mother of five children, a Buddhist monk, and a police officer. Imagine that each one of these people asks God the same question. It could be about anything: What would be in the highest good for me to say or do as I walk past this beggar on the street? What is my true purpose in life? How can I best serve myself and the world? What should I say or do if someone yells at me or threatens me? What am I here to learn?

Regardless of the question, each person is going to hear something unique and personal just for them. The 6-year-old child will not receive the same answer as the rebellious teenager, the Catholic priest, or the police officer. The mother of five will hear something different than the physicist or Buddhist monk. Each person has their own background, education, and belief systems. Each one is learning their own unique lessons in life. Because the purpose of God's Voice is to remind us of the Truth of Who We Are—restoring our awareness to Love—each one needs to hear something uniquely personal and intimate for their situation in order to bring about this shift in experience. Each person must be spoken to exactly where they are on their path of learning and growth. One person may be learning about kindness or compassion, while another person may be learning about forgiveness, abundance, or self-empowerment. What one person needs to hear to re-connect with their true Self will be different than what another person needs to hear.

In addition, we are constantly evolving and changing in our understanding and awareness. The lessons we were learning ten years ago are likely different than the lessons we are learning today. In fact, who we are in this moment is different than who we were three months ago, three weeks ago, and even three days ago. Each time we open up to a deeper understanding and experience of Love, Peace, Truth, or any other aspect of God, the fabric of our mind changes. We could ask God the same question each year for the rest of our lives and likely receive a different answer every time because what we are learning and assimilating in each moment is different. What we need to hear *right now* to be restored to the awareness of our true Self is unique to this moment. This makes each answer to our questions a tailor-made gift for each of us. **This is the 2ⁿᵈ key to hearing God's Voice—the Holy Spirit speaks to us exactly where we are on our path.**

The 3ʳᵈ Key to Hearing God's Voice

The 3ʳᵈ key to hearing God's Voice is the idea that Holy Spirit uses our background, life experience, personality, education, and everything about us to speak to us and through us in the world.

To explain, let's return to our previous example. Imagine that a 6-year-old child, a physicist, a Catholic priest, a rebellious teenager, a mother of five children, a Buddhist monk, and a police officer all ask God what would be in the highest good for he or she to say or do when walking past a beggar on the street.

Not only will each person receive a unique message and be spoken to exactly where they are in their learning and growth to restore their awareness to God, each one will also be spoken to in a way that he or she can personally understand and assimilate best. The 6-year-old child may receive communication using very simple words and ideas, while the Catholic priest may be inspired using biblical references and Christian terminology. Holy Spirit may remind the mother of five that all of God's children are equal, while the Buddhist monk may be inspired to see the beggar as himself, blessing him or her for the courage to learn about surrender and nonattachment to material possessions.

Based upon each person's unique background, life experience, personality, education, and all of the many other facets of their mind, each person will be spoken to in whatever manner and vocabulary is most appropriate for him or her. If someone enjoys gardening, Holy Spirit may communicate using gardening analogies. If someone is interested in science, Holy Spirit may communicate using that person's scientific understanding and vocabulary. **This is the 3rd key to hearing God's Voice—Holy Spirit uses our background, life experience, personality, education, and everything about us as a means to express to us and through us in the world.**

Once again, the 1st key to hearing God's Voice is the Holy Spirit is not outside of you. It is not a separate Being or Entity. It is the part of YOU that shares the awareness of God, the part of your own mind that sees yourself, the world, and everything in it through the eyes of God. The 2nd key is the Holy Spirit speaks to us where we are. The 3rd key is the Holy Spirit uses our background, life experience, personality, education, and everything about us to speak to us and through us in the world.

As you deepen your understanding and experience of these keys in the upcoming exercises, you will release the unconscious beliefs you hold within your mind that cause you to experience being separate from God and Holy Spirit. You will no longer need to compare what you hear from God's Voice within you to what another person hears within them. You will know that the communication, guidance, and insight you receive in each moment is exactly what *you* need to hear, regardless of the form, vocabulary, or style in which you receive it. And you will have a simple and direct way to hear God's Voice within you in a clear and recognizable way.

EXERCISE
Express God's Voice using Pen and Paper

In a previous exercise, we held the intention to hear God's Voice in any form it was given. In this exercise, we're going to hold the intention to hear specific words within us. As before, we'll begin with *Step 1: Extend Love to Your Thoughts*. Once we find ourselves in that quiet place within, we'll proceed to *Step 2: Feel God's Voice* and *Step 3: Ask a Question*. This time, instead of listening for an answer in whatever form it is given, we are going to give the part of our Self that *is* God's Voice a way to manifest words in the world using pen and paper.

Let me paint a picture for you. Imagine yourself going through this process: You're sitting in a comfortable chair with pen and paper in hand. Your eyes are closed and you're extending Love to whatever you become aware of. After a while, your "thoughts" start to melt away. Basking in that peaceful and comforting experience, you begin to feel God's Voice within you. Joined with that Presence, you feel deeper and deeper into it, allowing your experience of God's Voice to expand and strengthen. Although you feel as if you could stay in that experience of union all day, you decide to ask a question. Sometimes you ask questions aloud. In this moment, you simply ask the question silently within. With your attention firmly fixed on feeling that Presence of Love within you, you rest your pen on the piece of paper in front of you and ask your question. You have no idea what the answer will be, but you understand that **the words will come to you as soon as you start moving your pen**, so that's exactly what you do. You take a leap of faith and start moving your pen. The instant you do, you immediately become aware of a stream of thoughts and you begin to write them down as if you're dictating a letter to yourself. More questions come to you, and you write the answers down right behind them. After a while, you feel complete and set your pen down. What you've written feels true to you. It touches you deeply and you are filled with a profound sense of peace, understanding, and connection.

The process I just described is exactly what you're going to do in the next exercise. Receiving clear guidance and direction from God's Voice within you can truly be that simple. Before you get started, however, let me clarify a few things.

First, **it's important to extend Love to your thoughts throughout this entire process.** If thoughts of fear, judgment, doubt, confusion, or any other thoughts of the ego come to mind at any time, extend Love to them to keep yourself connected and in your Right-Mind along the way. If you ever need to restore your awareness of feeling God's Voice, go back to **Step 2: Feel God's Voice**, and then return to Steps 3 and 4 when you're ready.

In addition, when it's time to begin writing, **it's very important that you just get your hand moving.** You will likely not know what you're going to write before you start moving your hand because you haven't yet given Holy Spirit the use of your body as a means to express words to you. You must give that part of your Self the use of your body in order to manifest words in the world.

Remember, you are not "channeling" some other being or entity. You are not "bringing through" something "other" than your Self. You are getting in touch with the deepest part of YOU that shares the awareness of God and giving that part of your Self a way to express and manifest words in the world using your body.

Because Holy Spirit is not a separate being or entity, no one else besides you is going to move your pen and start writing. No other force or energy besides your own is going to move your pen. It is YOU who must take that leap of faith and start writing. **The moment you move your pen—not knowing what you're going to write—is the moment you actually commit to expressing God's Voice.** Do not wait for "something else" to move your pen. Do not wait to hear words or thoughts being spoken to you in your mind before you start writing. Just move your pen and the Holy Spirit's Consciousness will immediately be there to communicate to you in words using your pen and paper.

1. **Step 1: Extend Love to Your Thoughts** until you find yourself in the quietness of your Right-Mind.

2. **Step 2: Feel God's Voice** within you. Use gratitude as a bridge if you wish.

3. **Step 3: Ask a Question** when you're ready. It can be a specific question or a general question.

4. **Step 4: Express Gods Voice** in writing using a pen in the space provided on the following pages. You can write with your eyes open or closed, whichever feels more comfortable to you. Don't wait to hear words within you before you start writing. Just start writing and the words will immediately be there.

5. Feel free to ask as many questions as you like. When you feel complete, answer the questions that follow as thoroughly as possible.

YOUR QUESTION:

_____

_____

_____

_____

_____

ANSWER:

_____

_____

_____

_____

_____

_____

_____

_____

_____

_____

_____

_____

_____

_____

YOUR QUESTION:

_____

_____

_____

_____

_____

ANSWER:

_____

_____

_____

_____

_____

_____

_____

_____

_____

_____

_____

_____

_____

_____

_____

DESCRIBE YOUR EXPERIENCE

1. What was your experience of extending Love to your thoughts? Please describe.

_____

_____

_____

_____

_____

_____

_____

_____

_____

_____

_____

_____

_____

_____

_____

_____

_____

_____

_____

_____

_____

_____

2. What did God's Voice feel like? Please describe.

3. If you wrote down a message from God's Voice, how does the message make you feel? Please describe. If you did not experience receiving a message, what thoughts and feelings did you have while doing the exercise? Did you remember to extend Love to them during the exercise? If not, please do so after describing your thoughts and feelings below.

_____

_____

_____

_____

_____

_____

_____

_____

_____

_____

_____

_____

_____

_____

_____

_____

_____

_____

4. How has your experience shifted or changed as a result of receiving the message? Please describe.

How Do You Know?

Two common questions people ask when learning to hear God's Voice are: "How do I know if I'm really hearing God's Voice?" and "How do I know that I'm hearing God's Voice and not the ego's voice?"

The answer to these questions is simple. There are only two voices in the world—the voice of the ego and the Voice of God. Each voice represents a unique thought system. The thought system of the ego is based upon judgement, fear, and separation. The thought system of the Holy Spirit is based upon unconditional love. We are either thinking with one thought system or the other in any given moment.

If what you hear is filled with judgment, fear, sadness, anger, frustration, confusion, hopelessness, or anything else that is painful and causes you to feel separate, even if it's subtle, you can know you are hearing the voice of the ego. If what you hear brings you peace, love, happiness, acceptance, understanding, patience, forgiveness, joy, or any other state of mind that makes you feel good, connected, complete, and whole just as you are, you can know you are hearing the Voice of God.

This simple litmus test can be applied to everything you think, feel, and experience within you. If what you perceive is loving and kind, you can know you are hearing God's Voice. It is not possible for the ego to extend peace, compassion, forgiveness, or any other quality of God. That is not the ego's purpose. The thought system of the ego is only capable of instilling a sense of fear, judgment, or separation in one form or another. It is only your Right-Mind that has the power to bring about a sense of peace, love, connection, and wholeness in your life. If the communication, insight, inspiration, or guidance you receive helps to restore you to your true nature, you can rest assured that you are hearing and thinking with your Right-Mind.

How do you know when you're hearing God's Voice and not your own voice?

The truth is … you don't have your own voice. There are only two voices in the world, not three. There is the voice of the ego and the Voice of God. There is not the ego's voice, God's Voice, *and your voice.* The person you think you are in the world, which may be called John, Susan, Peter, or any other name, is made up of billions upon billions of thoughts that together form your personality, life experience, beliefs, goals, physical form, and everything else about who you appear to be in the world. This massive compilation of thoughts is NOT Who You *Are.* This vast collection of thoughts is simply an expression. You don't have your own voice. What you do have is an expression—your own unique expression—made up of billions upon billions of thoughts that you sometimes think is "you." The "person" who you appear to be in the world is your expression, not your Identity.

As an extension of God, you have complete freedom to choose which voice you want to hear and share in the world through your unique expression. Do you want to express Love? Or do you want to express fear? That is the choice you make in every moment. Each moment that you express fear or judgment, you are hearing and sharing the voice of the ego. Each moment that you express Love, or any other quality of God, you are hearing and sharing the Voice of God. There are an infinite number of expressions that God's Voice can take in the world. If what you hear is filled with Love, or any derivative of Love, you can know you are hearing God's Voice—**your own True Voice in the world.**

Step 5

Embody God's Voice

Step 5: Embody God's Voice

It is common to go through the **5 Steps to Hearing God's Voice**, receive clear life-altering communication, feel totally connected and at peace, and then forget to extend Love to all of the little thoughts and beliefs that bubble up within the mind *afterwards* that say, "Was that really God's Voice? Who do you think you are to believe you can hear God's Voice? I probably just made that up. Who knows if I'm even doing this correctly? Maybe that was just positive thinking," and all of the other countless thoughts of the ego that judge, belittle, dismiss, fear, or doubt what we just experienced, received, and did.

We are in the habit of listening to and believing these little thoughts of the ego. We've been listening to and believing them all our lives. How many times have you heard this Voice for Love within you, felt inspired to say or do something in your life, or known what was true for you in your heart, and then a little thought of doubt, judgement, or disbelief popped into your mind and you suddenly dismissed everything you heard or thought just a moment before? You may have even had a profound moment of hearing God's Voice in your life yet immediately began questioning your experience until you eventually judged it or doubted it into oblivion. Most of us have given these little thoughts of the ego enough power and meaning in our lives that when they float by within our mind, we unconsciously grab onto them, believe them, and make them our reality.

To address this habit and help you fully receive your experience of hearing God's Voice, it's important to include **Step 5: Embody God's Voice** *every time* you recognize or practice hearing God's Voice in your life. It is composed of three parts.

PART 1: Take in the message you just received.

It's common to receive communication and guidance from the Voice of God within us yet only absorb a fraction of its true meaning and implications for us. Spend some time "taking in" the communication you just received. Allow the message to sink deeper into your heart and mind. Feel the communication within you. Allow yourself to experience your oneness with the message you received. Just as you feel God's Voice in **Step 2: Feel God's Voice**, practice the same process with the communication, guidance, and answers you receive. *Be with* the communication. Feel it. Allow yourself to experience your oneness with it. Imagine that the communication is washing over and absorbing into every aspect of your consciousness, every fiber of your being, every cell of your body. In doing so, you allow yourself to fully receive the communication and guidance you have been given. Practice this part every time you hear God's Voice, regardless of the communication's form or expression. You may be surprised what occurs when you do. When you're done with Part 1, proceed to Part 2 below.

PART 2: Validate what you just did.

After you take in the message you just received, it's important to consciously acknowledge that you just heard God's Voice. The more you validate the fact that you just heard God's Voice, the more real it will become to you. Verbally say to yourself, "I just heard God's Voice," or "Thank you, God, for that message."

If you want to deepen your experience of hearing God's Voice, it's essential to acknowledge and validate that you are actually doing it. You *are* hearing God's Voice! Take that truth into your heart and mind.

You have been wanting to hear this Voice within you for a long time. It's not trivial, insignificant, or something to nonchalantly dismiss. Validate what you just did and really give that gift to yourself. Feel the gratitude you have for your relationship with God, for your ability to hear God's Voice, and for the communication you just received. When you acknowledge, validate, and feel your gratitude for what you just received, you transform your experience of hearing God's Voice from "something you want" to "something you have." After you complete Part 2, proceed to Part 3 below.

PART 3: Extend Love to every thought that tries to take away your experience.

When first learning to hear God's Voice, Part 3 may be the most important part of **Step 5: Embody God's Voice**. Be vigilant in extending Love to every thought that arises within you that tries to belittle, dismiss, invalidate, deny, or take away your experience of hearing God's Voice on any level. These types of thoughts may be so subtle that you barely notice them—a hint of doubt, a sense of unworthiness, a sliver of uncertainty about which voice you are hearing. Each time you extend Love to these thoughts of the ego, you heal the part of your mind that attempts to keep you from hearing God's Voice and you simultaneously strengthen the reality that you can and do hear this Voice in your life.

Extending love to thoughts of the ego is something that's important to do throughout every step of this 5 Step process, including all three parts of **Step 5: Embody God's Voice**. Anytime a thought of judgment, doubt, unworthiness, or any other thought of the ego arises within your mind to take away your experience of joining with God and receiving divine communication, extend Love, Compassion, Understanding, or a Blessing to that thought. Extending love in this way will keep you from innocently believing those tiny thoughts of the ego. The moment you believe them, they will become real to you and your experience of hearing God's Voice will disappear. It will be as if it never happened. In your mind, you will have made it up, made a mistake, misperceived, or had no idea what you were doing. That's how quickly your experience can change when you believe those tiny, seemingly insignificant thoughts of the ego. The moment you extend Love to them instead, however, you reclaim that meaning and power for your Self.

Remember, you give your thoughts all the meaning they have for you. It's the way you relate to your thoughts that gives you your experience, not the thoughts themselves. When you extend Love to the ego's thoughts, you see them for what they really are and they no longer need to become your reality. Extend love to your thoughts throughout this entire process. If you do, you will continue to melt away everything that keeps you from hearing God's Voice in your life and simultaneously drive yourself ever deeper into the life-changing experience of your union with God.

Important Note: If you didn't experience receiving communication from God's Voice in the last exercise, it's still critical to do all three parts of **Step 5: Embody God's Voice.** Doing so will assist you in opening up to hearing God's Voice more fully. If you didn't experience receiving a message, follow these instructions for each part below.

For Part 1 of Step 5, imagine that you *are receiving* Holy Spirit's communications to you on some level of Consciousness and that the communications are, in fact, seeping deeper and deeper into your mind even though you are not fully aware of them.

For Part 2 of Step 5, validate what you *are doing.* For example, you're learning how to relate to your thoughts and emotions in a loving way. You're learning to connect with and feel God's

Voice within you. You're doing a great job taking the necessary steps to open up to hearing God's Voice more clearly in your life. Acknowledge and give thanks for all the positive steps you *are taking*, and have faith that your day of consciously experiencing God's Voice in your life is coming soon.

For Part 3 of Step 5, extend Love, Understanding, Compassion, and Kindness to yourself and to any frustration, self-judgment, anger, or any other thought or emotion of the ego that tries to convince you that you are unworthy, incapable, it will never happen for you, or that everything isn't exactly as it should be. The disappointment, sadness, aloneness, or hurt that you may feel can only come from the ego. The Holy Spirit is not capable of giving you those emotions. Be mindful of your experience and extend Love to everything that arises that would cause you to feel separate from God. You can even extend gratitude for the opportunity to allow all of these buried thoughts and feelings to rise to the surface of your mind so they can be acknowledged and healed within you.

Every time you extend Love to whatever arises on the topic of hearing God's Voice, you clear away just a little more room within you to experience God's Voice in your life. So whether you experience receiving communication from God's Voice or not, practice all three parts of **Step 5: Embody God's Voice** every time and your experience of hearing God's Voice will surely strengthen.

EXERCISE
The 5 Steps to Hearing God's Voice

The more you practice hearing God's Voice, the stronger and more real your experience of this Voice will become. By finishing every practice session with **Step 5: Embody God's Voice**, you will eventually dissolve every sense of doubt and fear within you about hearing God's Voice. When you do, the clarity and certainty you have in joining with and hearing this Voice in the world will be undeniable, and you will have access to all the inner guidance and direction you need to fulfill your true purpose in the world. Continue to practice this process by following the 5 Steps below. Your experience of hearing God's Voice will deepen and strengthen each time you do.

1. **Step 1: Extend Love to Your Thoughts**.
2. **Step 2: Feel God's Voice**.
3. **Step 3: Ask a Question**.
4. **Step 4: Express Gods Voice**. Write the messages you receive in the space provided on the following pages. If any doubt, fear, judgment, or any other thoughts of the ego come up at any point in this process, return to Step 1 and extend Love to those thoughts, re-establish your connection, and then continue with the process. Repeat Steps 3 and 4 until you feel complete.
5. **Step 5: Embody God's Voice**. Part 1: Take in the message you just received. Part 2: Validate what you just did. Part 3: Extend Love to every thought that tries to take away your experience. When you are done, answer the following questions as thoroughly as possible.

QUESTION:

_____

_____

_____

_____

_____

ANSWER:

_____

_____

_____

_____

_____

_____

_____

_____

_____

_____

_____

_____

_____

_____

_____

QUESTION:

_____

_____

_____

_____

_____

ANSWER:

_____

_____

_____

_____

_____

_____

_____

_____

_____

_____

_____

_____

_____

_____

_____

_____

DESCRIBE YOUR EXPERIENCE

1. What was your experience of extending Love to your thoughts? Please describe.

_____

_____

_____

_____

_____

_____

_____

_____

_____

_____

_____

_____

_____

_____

_____

_____

2. What did God's Voice feel like? Please describe.

3. If you wrote down a message from God's Voice, how does the message make you feel? Please describe. If you did not experience receiving a message, what thoughts and feelings did you have while practicing the exercise? Did you remember to extend Love to them during the exercise? If not, please do so after describing your thoughts and feelings below.

_____

_____

_____

_____

_____

_____

_____

_____

_____

_____

_____

_____

_____

_____

_____

_____

_____

STEP 5: EMBODY GOD'S VOICE

Part 1. Spend a few minutes taking in the message you just received. Feel it. Be with it. Allow it to fill your heart and mind. How has your experience shifted or changed as a result of receiving the message? Please describe.

Part 2. Acknowledge and validate what you just did. You just received a message from the Voice of God within you! How does it feel?

Part 3. Do you notice any thoughts of doubt, fear, unworthiness, judgment, or any other thoughts of the ego bubbling up within your awareness to try to invalidate or take your experience away from you? If so, what thoughts and feelings do you notice? Write them down below and then extend Love, Compassion, Understanding, and/ or Forgiveness to them. How does extending Love to these thoughts change your experience of what you just did and the message you received?

Part Two

Becoming God's Voice in the World

EXERCISE
Speak God's Voice Out Loud

There is little difference between giving your Right-Mind a pen and paper to write with and opening your mouth and speaking God's Voice into the world. The process is exactly the same until the very last step. Instead of expressing your Self using a pen to manifest words on paper, you express your Self using your mouth to speak words out loud.

For some people, writing God's words onto paper is easier than speaking them, while for others opening their mouth and allowing the words to flow through them feels more natural. In a workshop my wife and I once conducted in Bellingham, Washington, a gentleman wrote only one word during the journaling exercise we did for **Step 4: Express God's Voice**. The word he wrote was, *"Wait."* Because it was a short workshop, we didn't have time to guide the participants through speaking God's Voice out loud, so we encouraged everyone to try it on their own when they got home. The gentlemen left the workshop feeling disappointed that he had only received one word. Three days later, we met up with him in British Columbia, Canada. He was beaming with joy! He went home after the workshop and practiced speaking God's Voice out loud. To his surprise, the words flowed effortlessly when he opened his mouth. He said that speaking God's Voice out loud was one of the most profound and impacting experiences of his life and that it felt easier and more natural for him than writing the words on paper. This is my personal experience as well.

There are truly no limits to how we can express God's Voice in the world. Whether we are speaking this Voice out loud while walking in nature, typing God's words on a keyboard, painting messages or pictures onto a piece of canvas, or singing beautiful songs while playing the guitar, we are expressing the same Voice for Love in the world. God's loving Voice is constant. What is continually changing is our expression of it.

In the following exercise, you will practice expressing God's Voice out loud. You will extend Love to your thoughts, feel this Voice within you, ask a question, and then give this part of your Self a way to manifest words in the world. In the previous writing exercise, I asked you to take a leap of faith by moving your hand, even if you didn't know what you were going to write. In this exercise, I'm going to ask you to take the same leap of faith by simply opening your mouth and starting to speak, even if you don't know what you're going to say. I don't mean that you're going to open your mouth and start talking gibberish or speaking in tongues, but what would you do if someone unexpectedly asked you to stand up at a wedding and give a toast or say grace at dinner? You would probably feel nervous, but you would stand up, take a deep breath, open your mouth, and just start speaking from your heart. You wouldn't necessarily know beforehand what you were going to say, but you would open your mouth and trust that whatever came out would be perfect. This is essentially what I'm asking you to do in this next exercise.

Go through the 5 Steps. In **Step 2: Feel God's Voice**, *be* in your heart. Feel this Presence of Love that you *are*. Join with this part of your Self that *is* God's Voice. Feel this aspect of your Divine Self within your upper body, head, and throat area. Allow yourself to BE the Holy Spirit in form. Then, when you're ready, ask your question. While you continue to experience feeling and *being* this Voice of Love that you truly *are*, open your mouth and start speaking. Remember, no one else is going to open your mouth for you. No other entity or being is going to come through your body. You are simply giving your Right-Mind a throat and vocal cords with which to manifest words in the world. *Be* your True Divine Self, open your mouth, and allow the words to flow freely.

Follow the 5 Steps below to experience speaking God's Voice out loud.

1. **Step 1: Extend Love to Your Thoughts.**
2. **Step 2: Feel God's Voice.**
3. **Step 3: Ask a Question.**
4. **Step 4: Express Gods Voice.** Open your mouth and share God's Voice out loud. Don't wait until you hear words within you before you open your mouth and start speaking. Just open your mouth with the intention to speak God's Voice and the words will immediately be there.

   If any doubt, fear, judgment, or any other thoughts of the ego arise within your mind at any point in this process, return to Step 1 and extend Love to those thoughts, re-establish your connection, and then continue with the process. Repeat Steps 3 and 4 until you feel complete.

   If you have a digital voice recorder, I recommend that you record yourself so you can listen to the message again later. If you don't have a way to record yourself, write your questions and answers on the following two pages when you're done to help you remember them later.
5. **Step 5: Embody God's Voice.** Part 1: Take in the message you just received. Part 2: Validate what you just did. Part 3: Extend Love to every thought that tries to take away your experience. When you are done, answer the following questions as thoroughly as possible.

QUESTION:

_____

_____

_____

_____

_____

ANSWER:

_____

_____

_____

_____

_____

_____

_____

_____

_____

_____

_____

_____

_____

_____

QUESTION:

_____

_____

_____

_____

_____

ANSWER:

_____

_____

_____

_____

_____

_____

_____

_____

_____

_____

_____

_____

_____

_____

_____

DESCRIBE YOUR EXPERIENCE

1. **What was your experience of extending Love to your thoughts? Please describe.**

_____

_____

_____

_____

_____

_____

_____

_____

_____

_____

_____

_____

_____

_____

_____

_____

_____

_____

_____

2. **What does your True Self feel like? Please describe.**

3. If you shared God's Voice out loud, what was it like? How did it feel? How was the experience different from journaling? Please describe. If you did not share a message out loud, what thoughts and feelings did you have while practicing the exercise? Did you remember to extend Love to them during the exercise? If not, please do so after describing your thoughts and feelings below.

_____

_____

_____

_____

_____

_____

_____

_____

_____

_____

_____

_____

_____

_____

_____

_____

_____

_____

_____

STEP 5: EMBODY GOD'S VOICE

Part 1. Spend a few minutes taking in the message you just received. Feel it. Be with it. Allow it to fill your heart and mind. How has your experience shifted or changed as a result of receiving the message? Please describe.

_____

_____

_____

_____

_____

_____

_____

_____

_____

_____

_____

_____

_____

_____

_____

_____

_____

_____

_____

_____

_____

_____

Part 2. Acknowledge and validate what you just did. You just received a message from God's Voice within you! How does it feel?

Part 3. Do you notice any thoughts of doubt, fear, unworthiness, judgment, or any other thoughts of the ego trying to invalidate your experience? If so, what thoughts and feelings do you notice? Write them down below and then extend Love, Compassion, Understanding, and/or Forgiveness to them. How does extending Love to these thoughts change your experience of what you just did and the message you received?

_____

_____

_____

_____

_____

_____

_____

_____

_____

_____

_____

_____

_____

_____

_____

_____

_____

_____

_____

Hearing God's Voice in All Ways

Hearing God's Voice is much more than hearing words within us. We are "hearing God's Voice" every time we think a loving thought, share a hug with a friend, smile at someone walking down the street, or thank the cashier at the grocery store. Hearing God's Voice encompasses all forms of giving and receiving love. When we believe that hearing God's Voice is limited to hearing a loud or audible voice in our heads, we deny ourselves the experience of hearing God's Voice in countless other ways.

When I first began hearing God's Voice in a conversational way, I thought I'd be in dialogue with this Voice from sunup to sundown, asking questions and seeking guidance with every step I took. As time went on, however, I began to realize that the joy, love, and fulfillment I was feeling was not only from hearing the words themselves but from experiencing my connection and union with God in the process. Hearing the words was fantastic and life-changing. They gave form and expression to my relationship with God in a very practical way. As my relationship with God continued to evolve and deepen, however, I came to see that I could connect with God and receive His love and communication in many different ways and that each form or expression of God's love gave me something just as uniquely fulfilling as hearing God's words alone could offer me.

Imagine being in a committed, long-term relationship with someone you love, yet the only form of communication you're able to have is the ability to write letters back and forth with one another. You're unable to speak to each other. There's no kissing, touching, or cuddling. You can't curl up on the couch and watch a good movie or read a book together. You can't give each other gifts, perform acts of kindness, or serve one another in any other way. You can't even rock back and forth in silence together on your front porch swing. All you can do to connect and communicate with one another is to write messages on paper.

I don't know about you, but I would want a lot more out of my relationship than just that. I wouldn't want to have only one form of communication and connection between us. Even if we enjoyed the most amazing conversations on paper and could write about anything we wanted, I would still want to experience some form of physical connection and intimacy. I would still want to spend quality time together doing things that nourished our relationship. I would still want to give and receive with one another in a variety of ways.

As human beings, we enjoy giving and receiving love in many different ways. Each form adds a dimension to our experience that no other form can fulfill on its own. Hearing God's Voice in the world is similar because "hearing God's Voice" is not just about communication. It's about developing a relationship with God. It's about giving and receiving love in all the ways that nurture our soul.

In some moments it can be very rewarding and practical to be able to receive explicit communication and guidance from Holy Spirit in actual words. In other moments, hearing specific words may not be necessary or even desirable. In certain situations you may want to ask God for a sign. In other situations you may want to simply sit in silence, feel God's Love, read a book, or speak to a friend as a way to connect with God or gain insight and understanding about a challenge you're facing. Each expression of God's Voice touches your heart in unique ways. Each one fulfills a need within you to experience God's Love in its totality. As a result, it's important to allow yourself to embrace and appreciate all forms of hearing God's Voice, not just a few.

In the end, it doesn't matter whether we hear specific words within us, become aware of a sign or symbol, perceive an inner vision, know in our hearts what to think or do next, or simply feel safe, loved, and complete just as we are. The end result of hearing God's Voice is always the same. Our relationship with God strengthens and we are brought ever deeper into the experience of God's Love for us.

Another important aspect of hearing God's Voice is the fact that the more we hear it, the more we start to recognize and experience our union with it. This shift in perspective is one of the greatest benefits to hearing God's Voice. The more we hear the Holy Spirit, the more we start to identify with it. This is equally true of extending love as well.

Because the Holy Spirit is the part of God that understands how to relate to the world while simultaneously knowing the Reality of God—the Reality of *Pure Being*—when we relate to our thoughts the way the Holy Spirit does, we are not only hearing God's Voice, we are also *being* God's Voice in that moment. This is why extending Love to our thoughts is such a powerful practice. Whether we perceive a thought to be "within our mind" or "out in the world," when we relate to our thoughts in a loving way, we are truly *being* the Holy Spirit in that moment. We are *being* what the Holy Spirit *is*—an extension of Love that perceives all of creation with Love.

Regardless of how you connect with, hear, or express God's Voice, being conscious of this connection has the power to create miracles in your life. When you're in your Right-Mind and conscious of your connection with God, you cannot help but experience the Presence of God wherever you are. You cannot help but see the Perfection of God in all things. You cannot help but be in Holy Relationship with everyone and everything. When you are in your Right-Mind, you have the power to receive everything you truly seek ... and it all begins with the simple act of extending Love to your thoughts.

Extending Love Without an Egoic Agenda

Nearly everyone who extends Love to their thoughts experiences the same dramatic results. Their thoughts suddenly disappear and they find themselves in a more quiet and peaceful state of mind. As a result, it's common for people to learn this technique, enjoy a new-found sense of peace and joy, and then innocently begin to use this process *in order to* make their thoughts go away.

It was said in Step 1 on page 25, "The ego judges every thought that goes through our mind: We either like it or we don't like it. We think it's a good thought or a bad thought, a spiritual thought or not-so-spiritual thought. We want to hold onto it or get rid of it. We believe it or we don't believe it. **The ego is always judging**. It is always determining what to do to a thought or with a thought. And if it's not immediately choosing to like it or dislike it, keep it or get rid of it, it's choosing to improve upon it, upgrade it, or make it better. This is the way the ego relates to thought, and it's always from a place of judgment, no matter how subtle that judgment may be."

From the ego's perspective, extending Love to our thoughts can be a wonderful new way to control our thoughts, manage our thinking, and get rid of the thoughts we don't like or want. When we hold the intention to extend Love *in order to* make our thoughts disappear, we are no longer "extending Love." We are using *the concept* of extending Love as a way for the ego to continue to judge and manipulate all that passes through our mind.

In the process of learning how to extend Love, there will be times when our intention is split. Part of us is truly extending love for its own sake, while another part is trying to improve or fix our experience because we don't like it or want it. When our intention is split and we extend Love *in part* with an egoic agenda, we won't experience the same dramatic results we normally would. Extending love in this way may placate us for awhile, but as time goes on, we'll realize that the profound peace, love, joy, and fulfillment we so deeply long for and experience when we usually extend Love is somehow missing.

When we authentically extend Love to our thoughts and emotions, we have no intention to make our thoughts and emotions go away. Instead, we fully acknowledge them, embrace them, accept them, and allow them to *be*. There is no judgment. We don't need to improve upon them or change them. We simply join "what is," with love and acceptance in our heart and mind. When we extend Love to our thoughts and emotions with no other intention than to simply *be* in Holy Relationship with them, they naturally dissolve and fall away, not because we want them to but because we join them at the level of *being* where all things are One. This is when true healing occurs.

To authentically practice the process of extending Love, it's important to notice when you are extending love with an egoic agenda. When you become aware that you are extending Love to a person, situation, emotion, or thought in order to make it go away, fix it, or achieve a certain result, notice that intention and then extend a little smile, understanding, compassion, or love to it. Doing so will free you to reconnect with what you truly seek in your heart, which is the opportunity to experience true love, true connection, and true peace. Once you've reconnected with that love within you, return your attention to the person, situation, emotion, or thought you were originally trying to extend Love to. This time, extend Love for its own sake. Extend love because you want to experience what it's like to *be* in a holy and loving relationship with that thought. You aren't trying to achieve anything. You aren't trying to make anything happen. You aren't trying to make anything go away. You simply want to experience true love, true peace, and true union because that is what you long for more than anything else. When you extend Love with that holy intention, your thoughts will suddenly disappear and you'll find yourself in a more quiet and peaceful state of mind.

All Thoughts Serve the Same Purpose

Extending Love to your thoughts can feel very natural and easy when the thoughts you're extending Love to contain very little emotional charge or hold no meaning for you. Eventually, however, there will come a time when something arises within you that you don't want to extend Love to because you experience that "something" as wrong, painful, unjust, rude, mean, insensitive, attacking, unacceptable, or some other quality of the ego that you "know" to be true. For most of us, if we have a strong emotional reaction to something, we usually don't perceive our experience to simply be the result of a "thought" we are holding within our mind. To us, the story we've written is real.

Have you ever said or heard anything like this before? "I have proof. It's what really happened. What that person said or did really is wrong, unjust, rude, mean, insensitive, or unacceptable. Everyone would agree."

That is the power of thought. The thoughts we think we may come to believe. What we believe becomes true in our experience. What we experience to be true shapes our world and the way we see it.

When we identify with and literally *become* the emotionally charged thoughts we think, it's easy to believe that extending Love to our thoughts has no value or real-world application to it, but that's precisely when we need to extend Love the most. The more you practice extending Love to your painful emotions, the more conviction you'll have in the power of extending Love when the going gets tough. **Remember, all**

thoughts serve the same purpose. They give you the opportunity to extend Love. Whether you're extending Love to a physical sensation, belief, judgment, emotion, person, situation, yourself, or an indefinable string of thoughts and feelings all bunched together like a ball of yarn within you, the outcome is the same—you feel connected, whole, and peaceful once again.

When you find yourself in pain, struggling, upset, and in the throes of the ego's way of thinking, even if you're a hundred percent convinced your position is right and justified, ask yourself, "Would I rather be right, or would I rather be happy?" It's one or the other. You can't have both. In the moment that you choose to extend Love to your thoughts instead of choosing to be right, you will create profound miracles in your life.

The more you practice extending Love to all things without discrimination, especially to the pain that feels the most real and justified to you, the quicker you'll come to know that you truly can count on God's Love to answer and resolve every question and challenge that arises in your life.

Looking Forward to the Opportunity

When you resist, judge, or avoid thoughts of the ego, you are already in the ego's way of thinking. When you look forward to noticing when thoughts of the ego arise within you, you are able to welcome them with an open heart and see them for what they truly are—an opportunity to extend Love.

The way you relate to the thoughts within you is the same way you relate to the thoughts you perceive to be outside of you "in the world."

The more easily you can allow all things to rise and pass away within you, the more easily you can allow all things to rise and pass away in the world. **Your relationship to the world is a reflection of your relationship to your thoughts.** The more peace you have with your thoughts, the more peace you will have in the world.

When you notice that you are judging the ego—resisting the fear, judgment, and pain within you—simply notice that you are relating to the ego's thoughts with the ego and extend Love to that judgment or resistance. Allow the ego to arise within your awareness. Allow the fear, anger, sadness, or pain within you to arise without judgment. Only by allowing the ego to exist are you able to authentically extend Love to it without judgment. Only by allowing it to exist are you able to embrace it with true love, compassion, understanding, and forgiveness. The more you practice allowing the ego to arise within your awareness, the more you will come to experience the gift that the ego truly is for you. The more you practice allowing the ego to exist, the more you will begin to look forward to the opportunity to acknowledge and embrace the ego with love. When you look forward to embracing the ego, you hold no resistance to it. Your heart is open and willing to embrace all things. Such openheartedness can only come from one place—Love. **Look forward to the opportunity to have the ego arise within your mind so you can shine the Love of God upon it and enter into a holy relationship with it.** It is this holy opportunity that allows you to restore the fragments of your mind to the wholeness and oneness of God's Love within you. It is this opportunity that allows you to fulfill your true purpose in the world.

The Many Flavors of Love

We use the word *Love* to describe the *essence* of who we *are* and what God *is*. We also use the word *Love* to describe our *experience of Pure Being*—what we experience in the absence of ego. The practice of *extending Love* gives us a simple and effective way to experience this state of *Being* by relating to all of creation *as* the Holy Spirit.

If you struggle with extending Love to your thoughts because you are uncertain what Love is or what Love feels like to you, it's important to remember that there are many flavors of Love to choose from. Instead of extending Love, you could extend Gratitude, Compassion, Kindness, Understanding, Gentleness, Acceptance, Blessings, or any other quality of God that you choose. The practice of extending Love gives you a way *to be* in Holy Relationship, but it doesn't ultimately matter which flavor of Love you hold in your heart when relating to your thoughts. If it's an aspect or quality of your *True Self*, the outcome will be the same, so choose whatever flavor of Love works best for you in any given moment.

A Way of Being

When people first learn to close their eyes and extend Love, they sometimes think they need to extend Love to every thought they notice. Before long, they find their meditations busier than ever and there is very little peace in the experience.

If you find the process of extending Love to be a busy one, know that you don't need to extend Love to every thought that comes into your mind. Extend love to one thought at a time in a relaxing and comfortable manner. There is no need to hurry. There is nowhere to go and nothing to accomplish. Feel free to take your time and enjoy the moment.

If you verbally bless every thought or visualize yourself sprinkling golden pixie dust on every thought, you may want to experiment with a more simplified expression of Love. Simply feeling your Love, for example, instead of adding words or pictures to the expression, can help to eliminate any busyness you might experience.

In the end, extending Love is more than an activity—it is truly a way of being. Approach it with this intention and the more divine and transforming your experience will be.

Being Present in the Now

The process of extending Love to your thoughts might begin as a mental exercise, but the longer you engage in this practice and the deeper you take it, the more it will become a quiet and peaceful state of being that requires only your gentle awareness. When this occurs, all that arises and falls away within your mind will be met with tenderness and open arms. A feeling of sadness or fear could arise within you, yet your connection and awareness of Pure Being will remain undisturbed. Though you may still perceive the feelings of ego, you will simultaneously feel the Love and vastness of your Being encompassing it. Your awareness will be rooted in Source, and there will be little or no distinction between the rising and falling away of thoughts and emotions, your extension of Love to them, and your experience of Pure Being. You will perceive it all, yet experience only Oneness.

While this may sound esoteric, the more you practice extending

Love to your thoughts and emotions in a state of meditation, the more often you will experience this way of being with your eyes open in the world. You will become acutely present with everything that unfolds in your life. Whether it's a belief, sensation, or judgment passing through your awareness, or the physical experience of working in your garden, speaking with someone you meet on the street, or gazing into another's eyes, you will simply be present with "what is" because your natural reaction to *all things* will be to acknowledge them, embrace them, and extend Love to them with no other intention than to simply BE in a loving relationship with them.

While the concept of extending Love to your thoughts may be simple in theory, the longer you practice it, the more profound it will become.

Extending Love in Conversation

Extending Love in the world can look and feel very differently from one situation to the next. There are no rules. Just begin whenever and however you can. As an example, let's say that you're having a difficult conversation with someone. It could be with your spouse, a co-worker, or with one of your clients or customers. If you find yourself getting emotional or feel as if you're about to say or do something you would rather not, take a deep breath and begin to extend Love to your thoughts, emotions, and to yourself to help you maintain your composure and reestablish your sense of connection with Self.

If you think the other person is struggling more than you, extend Love to them instead of yourself, or extend Love to the ideas and emotions they are trying to share with you. This will help you to stay present, listen to them with a more open mind, feel compassion for what they are going through, and have more empathy and understanding for what they truly want and need. The more you extend Love to whatever arises in the conversation, the smoother, more fulfilling, and more productive the conversation is likely to be.

If you do end up saying or doing something you wish you hadn't, extend compassion, love, and forgiveness to yourself and to any self-judgment that you feel. No matter what happens, gently remind yourself that **everything is an opportunity to extend Love.** The more you do it, the more loving, compassionate, clear, and connected you will experience being. You will just keep taking it deeper and deeper every time you extend Love because everything you ultimately want is a direct extension of the Love that you *are*.

EXERCISE
Make a Commitment

You can talk about extending love or hearing God's Voice all day, but unless you actually do it, you will experience little benefit from it. The more you practice the 5 Steps, the easier they will become, the more confident you will feel, and the more you will experience the Peace, Love, and understanding you desire.

If this is truly what you want in your life, make a commitment to yourself—right now—to practice these 5 Steps on a regular basis. It could be every morning when you wake up, during your lunch break at work, before turning on the TV at night, or any other time that works best for you. What's important is that you practice these steps in some way on a regular basis. The more you practice them, the more you will experience the results. The more you experience the results, the more you will come to believe, choose, apply, and integrate this "way of being" into your life.

To support yourself in making this commitment, take a few minutes to answer the following questions:

1. What can I do on a daily basis to strengthen my experience of hearing God's Voice in my life?

2. **What can I do on a weekly basis to strengthen my experience of hearing God's Voice in my life?**

_____

_____

_____

_____

_____

_____

_____

_____

_____

_____

_____

_____

_____

_____

_____

_____

_____

_____

_____

_____

_____

_____

_____

3. **What can I do on a monthly basis to strengthen my experience of hearing God's Voice in my life?**

_____

_____

_____

_____

_____

_____

_____

_____

_____

_____

_____

_____

_____

_____

_____

_____

_____

_____

_____

_____

_____

4. **What might keep me from following through with these commitments? List anything that comes to mind and then take a few minutes to extend Love to whatever you write down.**

_____

_____

_____

_____

_____

_____

_____

_____

_____

_____

_____

_____

_____

_____

_____

_____

_____

_____

_____

_____

_____

_____

5. What action do I need to take right now to follow through with these commitments? Write down whatever steps or actions you need to take and then take them.

_____

_____

_____

_____

_____

_____

_____

_____

_____

_____

_____

_____

_____

_____

_____

_____

_____

_____

_____

_____

_____

_____

_____

_____

EXERCISE
Deepening Your Experience of God's Voice

These are the **5 Steps to Hearing God's Voice**:

Step 1: Extend Love to Your Thoughts.

Step 2: Feel God's Voice.

Step 3: Ask a Question.

Step 4: Express God's Voice.

Step 5: Embody God's Voice.

Each step in this process has a specific purpose. **Step 1: Extend Love to Your Thoughts** restores you to your Right-Mind so you can more clearly hear God's Voice. **Step 2: Feel God's Voice** strengthens your overall experience of connection and union with this Voice. **Step 3: Ask a Question** sets the stage for receiving communication. **Step 4: Express God's Voice** gives your Right-Mind a way to manifest God's Voice in the world. You might give your Right-Mind a pen and paper to write words or draw pictures with, a tongue and vocal cords to speak or sing with, your unique personality to inspire and create with, or countless other means to express God's Voice in the world. **Step 5: Embody God's Voice** is the last step. It strengthens your overall experience of hearing, sharing, and *being* God's Voice in the world by helping you to 1) fully receive the gift that is given you; 2) acknowledge and validate what you are truly doing and being; and 3) extend Love to any thoughts of the ego that try to diminish or invalidate your experience in any way.

At this stage of learning, it's important to practice each step in order to strengthen and embody each individual skill. Over time, the steps will merge and become one. Similar to the idea of learning to swing a golf club, it's essential to learn and train each skill individually, i.e. how to hold the club, position your feet, move from your center, keep your eye on the ball, follow through, etc. With practice, the artificial separation between each skill falls away and all parts flow seamlessly as one fluid action. With practice, the **5-Steps to Hearing God's Voice** will become an effortless, seamless flow of one single action as well. Whenever you choose to receive or express God's Voice, the steps will become one fluid natural experience. You will simply think about hearing God's Voice and an experience of union and communication will instantly be there.

To deepen your experience of hearing this Voice, practice the 5 Steps again. Write your questions and answers in the space provided on the following pages. When you're done, answer the questions that follow. If you need additional clarification about these steps, refer to the previous exercises.

Step 1: Extend Love to Your Thoughts.
Step 2: Feel God's Voice.
Step 3: Ask a Question.
Step 4: Express God's Voice.
Step 5: Embody God's Voice.

QUESTION:

_____

_____

_____

_____

_____

ANSWER:

_____

_____

_____

_____

_____

_____

_____

_____

_____

_____

_____

_____

_____

_____

_____

QUESTION:

_____

_____

_____

_____

ANSWER:

_____

_____

_____

_____

_____

_____

_____

_____

_____

_____

DESCRIBE YOUR EXPERIENCE

1. What was your experience of extending Love to your thoughts? Please describe.

_____

_____

_____

_____

_____

_____

_____

_____

_____

_____

_____

_____

_____

_____

_____

_____

_____

_____

_____

_____

2. What did God's Voice feel like? Please describe.

3. If you wrote down a message from God's Voice, how does the message make you feel? Please describe. If you did not experience receiving a message, what thoughts and feelings did you have while practicing the exercise? Did you remember to extend Love to them during the exercise? If not, please do so after describing your thoughts and feelings below.

_____

_____

_____

_____

_____

_____

_____

_____

_____

_____

_____

_____

_____

_____

_____

_____

_____

STEP 5: EMBODY GOD'S VOICE

Part 1. Spend a few minutes taking in the message you just received. Feel it. Be with it. Allow it to fill your heart and mind. How has your experience shifted or changed as a result of receiving the message? Please describe.

_____

_____

_____

_____

_____

_____

_____

_____

_____

_____

_____

_____

_____

_____

_____

_____

_____

_____

_____

Part 2. Acknowledge and validate what you just did. You just received a message from the Voice of God within you! How does it feel?

_____

_____

_____

_____

_____

_____

_____

_____

_____

_____

_____

_____

_____

_____

_____

_____

_____

_____

_____

_____

_____

_____

_____

Part 3. Do you notice any thoughts of doubt, fear, unworthiness, judgment, or any other thoughts of the ego trying to invalidate your experience? If so, what thoughts and feelings do you notice? Write them down below and then extend Love, Compassion, Understanding, and/or Forgiveness to them. How does extending Love to these thoughts change your experience of what you just did and the message you received?

_____

_____

_____

_____

_____

_____

_____

_____

_____

_____

_____

_____

_____

_____

_____

_____

_____

_____

Part Three

Being God's Voice in the World

Experiencing Your Divine Self

Beginning on page 13, it was said that God is Love, or Pure Being, and that God is All That Is. God's Child, an extension of God and One with its Creator, invented the thought system of the ego as a way to experience what it would be like to be autonomous or separate from God. As this thought occurred, God created the Holy Spirit to act as a reminder within God's Child of the Truth of Who It Is. The Holy Spirit is able to accomplish this purpose because it shares in the full awareness of God while also having the ability to perceive and understand the thought system of the ego. The Holy Spirit can perceive everything that has ever been thought by the ego, but it doesn't believe it, and continues to hold Truth within the mind of God's Child.

This simple framework and understanding gives us, as the Child of God, a way to undo our belief in separation. It gives us a means to restore our attention and awareness to the Infinite and Absolute, to the experience of Love and Pure Being. It gives us a method to release all of the meaning, allegiance, belief, attachment, power, reality, and life-force that we have given to the thought system of the ego, so we can be restored in our awareness of being One with All That Is.

This transformation in awareness is exactly what has occured for me personally in practicing the 5 Steps and learning to integrate this Consciousness into my life, so much so in fact that the above framework is now dissolving within me, providing me with the most fulfilling, all-encompassing and perpetual experience of connection and Oneness I have ever known.

When I first experienced this framework starting to dissolve within me, I didn't share my experience with anyone except my wife. When I eventually told my students years later, it seemed to provoke misunderstanding, confusion, and uncertainty. Wanting to serve them "where they were," I stopped sharing my deepest understanding and experience of God with them, trusting that their practice of the 5 Steps would gently guide them to their own deeper understanding and experience of God at just the right time and place for them.

So why am I about to break my silence and share my experience with you now? For two reasons: First, I don't want to hold my experience inside any longer. It's an experience that impacts my life so deeply each and every day that I no longer want to keep it from those who seek a similar experience in their own lives, which leads me to my second reason. In looking at the subtitle of this book and then proceeding to read it, you made a decision that you already were or wanted to be, "On the Leading Edge of Consciousness." That's why I added the subtitle in the first place, so people would selectively weed themselves out from reading this book. Sure, you could be reading this out of curiosity or intrigue, but chances are, you truly long to experience the Truth of Who You *Are* at a level of depth and consistency that permeates your experience of life in every way, which is precisely what has occurred for me in practicing these 5 Steps and integrating them into my life. I therefore trust that these words have come to you at just the right time and place or you wouldn't be reading them now.

One final thing. What I'm about to share with you has been excluded from the other versions of this book. Why should I disturb or confuse those people who don't want to hear what I'm about to say? Just as the Holy Spirit joins people "where they are," it's my desire to do the same. So here we go:

In 1993, I unexpectedly experienced a profound moment of enlightenment. In that moment, every thought, belief, and judgment fell away and I experienced for the first time the Truth of Who I Am— the Truth that *I Am* Love and Love *is* All That Is. This instantaneous experience was so powerful that my personal sense of identity in the world literally disappeared before my eyes. All that was left was an experience of *being* the Love that *I Am*. I cried tears of joy for weeks on end, danced and sang in the streets, smiled from ear to ear all day long, and could barely contain the joy, peace, and utter celebration of life that I felt.

This ongoing experience lasted for about three months. Then one day while driving down the road in my car, I noticed a tiny thought of fear pass through my mind, and then another, and another. Spontaneously, the ego had somehow come back to life within me, and I didn't have a clue how to deal with it. Within a matter of months, my continual and all-encompassing experience of bliss was gone. All that remained was the memory of *What* I had experienced in those 3 months and the conviction that it was indeed possible to live *as* the Presence of Love in the world.

When this life-changing experience of utter joy and happiness faded from my life, I began to earnestly seek a way to hear God's Voice within me so I could learn how to reclaim that state of ongoing peace and joy. Several years of heart-wrenching ups and downs followed. Eventually I began hearing God's Voice in early 2000 with the help of my wife, Candace. Before long, I was connecting with this Voice for Love on a regular basis, asking lots of questions and sincerely applying the guidance and teachings I was given.

In 2005, after Candace and I wrote our first book, *The Voice for Love*, we were given the "5-Steps to Hearing God's Voice" from the Holy Spirit as a way to teach people how to hear God's Voice within them in our workshops. While traveling the country conducting workshops for nearly two straight years after the release of our book, we not only practiced the 5 Steps ourselves, we became truly dedicated to integrating them into our lives.

Somewhere along the way, something profound began to shift within me. **The more I integrated the process of extending Love, embracing my emotions, and joining with and experiencing God's**

Voice as my own True Voice, the deeper and deeper my experience of Oneness became.

I remember the first time I experienced my utter Oneness with God and the Holy Spirit while practicing the 5 Steps. One day while meditating, I noticed that I felt a little awkward asking God a question because I sensed deep within me that I was only asking my Self. I knew conceptually that I was One with God and the Holy Spirit, but I had always been able to perceive at least some level of distinction between God, God's Voice, and my Self. In that particular moment, I no longer could. All I experienced was, *"I Am God. I Am All That Is."*

I know that might sound like a stretch. For some, it may be acceptable to say, "I am One with God," but to say, "I Am God," that's entirely different, even blasphemous or downright insane. Before you interpret what I mean, please be patient for a moment and follow me through this:

Imagine that everything you see in the world is filled with tiny rays of Golden Light. Take a moment, right now, to visualize in your imagination that Golden Light is emanating within all of creation. This Light is the Essence of God—the Essence of Love and Pure Being. It permeates everything in existence, every thought, every desire, every emotion, and every physical object. Everything, on all levels of existence, is imbued with this Light, surrounded by this Light, radiating this light, and is an extension of this Light. Everything is literally made-up, or composed, of this Light.

The Light that I speak of goes by many names—God, Love, Spirit, Beingness, Existence, the Great I Am, Essence, Universal Energy, Life-Force, Cosmic Consciousness, Source—and many others. No matter WHAT it is called, it IS the very Light that you ARE. You *are* that Spirit. You *are* that *Beingness*. You *are* that *Love* ... and so is everything else in existence too. Whether it's a thought, a desire, an emotion, a body, a building, a mountain, or an entire universe, everything in existence simply *IS*, because everything in existence is made up of the Light that *IS* Beingness itself. This is why you literally *are* the Light of the world. You are not a body that lives and dies. You are the *Beingness* that permeates all of Creation. That is your True Identity and the reason why your True Self is Infinite, Eternal, Changeless, and Perfect—always.

Why don't we experience this Reality in our daily lives?

To answer this question, imagine that this infinite expanse of Golden Light is imbued with the Consciousness of Pure Being—the Consciousness of God. There is no distinction between the Light and the Consciousness of God. They are one and the same. If you were to experience this Consciousness directly, you would experience only the Peace, Love, and Joy of Infinite Being.

Now imagine that all of creation exists within this infinite expanse of Light. This would include both the thought system of the ego and the thought system of the Holy Spirit. ALL of creation takes place within this infinite expanse of Golden Light. Nothing can ever leave the Light or be separate from It. Because the Light equally encompasses all of creation, regardless of what seems to rise and pass away within the Light, the Light remains unchanged, undisturbed, and ever present. The Light simply IS.

Because this Light exists within you, the Consciousness of God exists within you as well. The Infinite and Eternal Beingness of God exists within you and within every thought, belief, emotion, and experience you have ever had. The Light of God exists within everyone and everything—always.

There are countless thoughts that collectively form our individual personalities, beliefs, interests, relationships, culture, and the physical world as we know it. When the thought system of the ego was invented, the features of "belief" and "attachment" were incorporated into it so the Light of Consciousness would have the opportunity to become identified with the thoughts of the ego. That was the purpose for creating the ego, to give Consciousness the opportunity to experience what it *would be like* to be autonomous or separate from Itself. In order to do that, it was essential for Consciousness to be able to become attached to, believe, and identify with the thoughts of the ego. This is why we "as Consciousness" experience, believe, and identify with the countless thoughts that collectively form our individual personalities, beliefs, interests, relationships, culture, and the physical world as we know it. The ego's thought system was specifically designed to accomplish that, and it does its job perfectly, just as we created it to do.

For those in the world who are listening to and following the Voice for Love within them, we are now collectively on our return journey of awakening together. We have already experienced the depths of what it *would be like* to be separate from our Self and are now restoring our awareness to our God Consciousness. We are now pulling all the meaning, reality, belief, allegiance, and life-energy out of the thought system of the ego so we can fully restore ourselves to our Right-Mind and thus wholly experience our True Nature once again.

To help you remember Who You truly *are*, let me share the following story with you again, just a little differently this time:

Before there was time and space, before the Earth or anything in the universe existed, there was God.

There are many great words to describe God: Father/Mother, Creator, Spirit, I Am That I Am, Cosmic Consciousness, Universal Mind, Divine Being, Unconditional Love, All That Is, Source, Infinite Wisdom, Essence of Life, the Great I Am ... The list could go on and on. For the sake of our description, we'll say that God *is* the Great *I Am*.

As the story goes, God is simply *being* all that God *is,* and God is extending It's Beingness infinitely in all directions, when suddenly, as if out of the blue, a thought rose up within the Mind of God that said something like, "What would it be like to become aware of my Self? What would it be like to Self-Realize my own Existence?"

Being as creative as God is, it's as if God scratched It's head and thought, "Hmmm, how could I possibly do that? How could I possibly Self-Realize my own Existence?"

In a flash God thought, "What if I could create a way of thinking that was so convincing and real that it gave Me the opportunity to consciously experience what it would be like to be other than *I Am*?"

So God did. God created a way of thinking that gave Itself the opportunity to experience what it would be like *to be* what God is NOT, and God called this way of thinking the "ego." That is all the ego is—a way of thinking that gives God the opportunity to experience what It is not.

When there is only Light, there is no darkness. Nothing else exists. **For God to truly know Itself as Light, It must first come to know Itself as darkness. There must be something "other than Light" to compare Itself with.** In this case, God invented the ego to be this "other." By first coming to identify with the darkness as Itself, God is able to turn back upon Itself and experience the Light of Who and What It truly Is.

Who can't look into a baby's eyes and see the very Presence of Love staring back? When a baby first comes into the world, its experience is one of Pure Being. There is no sense of self, no sense of separation from its mother or surroundings—just Being. As time goes on, the baby's Consciousness begins to lose this undifferentiated state of Being and starts to identify with its body and the thought system of the ego. Eventually, it will experience what it's like to feel alone, vulnerable, afraid, and hurt. With every passing year, the baby's identification with the ego continues to deepen. By the time it reaches adolescence, the baby has come to believe that he or she *is* the vast complexity of thoughts that define his or her experience of being loved or unloved, worthy or unworthy, successful or unsuccessful, and so on. Regardles of how long this ego identification lasts, there will eventually come a day when this grown baby (who is you) desires to re-experience its divine state of Love and Being once again. The pain of the ego has become too great, and the desire within you to realize and experience Who and What you truly *are* has been re-born.

This is the journey that you and every human being is on. No matter how far you travel down the road of rediscovering your True Self, **you already *are* all that you seek. You *are* God remembering your True Nature. You *are* God experiencing who and what you are NOT, so that you can fully realize Who and What you truly *are*.**

The state of being of a newborn baby and that of a Self-Realized Master are nearly identical—both simply *are* the Presence of Love in the world. The only difference between them is that the baby doesn't know it. The baby is unaware of who and what it is, while the awakened, self-realized Master *consciously experiences* its Beingness and knows that He or She *is* the Presence of God in expression—One with All That Is.

The cultivation and expression of this Self-Awareness is the Purpose of creation itself. Everything in the world serves this one Divine Purpose. Whether God appears to be going deeper and deeper into the thought system of the ego in order to experience what It is not, or whether God appears to be consciously extending Love and remembering Who and What It truly is, everything serves the same ultimate Purpose.

Self-Realization cannot be fulfilled without the ego. By first experiencing what you are not, you *as God* are able to open the door to the conscious experience of Who and What you truly *are*. The ego and the Holy Spirit work hand-in-hand to accomplish this round-trip journey. **The ego provides one leg of the journey, while the Holy Spirit provides the other. Only together is the journey of Self-Realization possible.**

In the process of awakening to one's True Nature, it is common to perceive the ego as separate from God. When one perceives through the eyes of the ego, how else could one experience the ego? When one fully recognizes that God is *All That Is*, this recognition naturally embraces the thought system of the ego as well. It is only the thought system of the ego that projects separation upon itself and cannot see the Love and Light that it *is*.

Every thought simply *is*. Every thought *is* God in expression. Some thoughts have the purpose of giving God the experience of what It is not. Other thoughts have the purpose of reminding God of the Truth of Who It is. Both thought systems serve God in becoming Self-Aware. Whether God is going deeper into the illusion or pulling Itself out, either way God is extending Love with every thought, because every thought literally *is* Love and is equally important in bringing God closer to the conscious realization of Its Infinite Nature. The push and the pull, the up and the down, the black and the white, the ego and the Holy Spirit ... they are all equal and necessary expressions of God because they are all ultimately leading God in the same direction of becoming Self-Actualized. Self-Realization cannot happen without both thought systems.

This is why the ego is equally as holy as the Holy Spirit. It does indeed have a divine function and purpose: to serve God in experiencing who and what It is not. **It is only when we think and perceive *with the ego* that we perceive the ego as bad, wrong, unholy, evil, or something to eradicate and defend ourselves against.** When we see through eyes of Love and Truth instead, the illusion of separation that the ego offers us simply melts away in our experience.

The Consciousness of God is infinite, and thus is yours. You do not experience God's Consciousness as your own because the tiny fragment of God's Consciousness that you experience as "you" is predominantly identified with the ego's way of thinking. As you continue to relate to the ego with love and thus release the ego's way of thinking from your mind, you will continue to restore your awareness to its Infinite Nature. The deeper you go into your own Infinite Consciousness, the more expansive your sense of Identity will become. Eventually you will come to experience your Self for Who and What you truly are.

You *are* all that you seek. Take this Truth to heart. When you find yourself lying in bed with the flu, extend Love to yourself and all the thoughts of the ego that would try to convince you that something is wrong. You *are* God experiencing the flu. If you can fully embrace and lovingly accept that experience, it may be one of the most enlightening moments of your life. When you find yourself sweating on a hot summer's day, feel the Divinity of Being God in form on a hot summer's day. Extend Love, Acceptance, Compassion, and Joy to all things, and Divinity will be yours in every moment.

Every thought and experience can be perceived through the eyes of the ego or through the eyes of Love. It is the way you relate to your thoughts that determines your experience. Relate to yourself and the world through the eyes of the ego and you will know the experience of fear, judgment, and separation. Relate to yourself and the world through the eyes of Love and you will know the experience of Peace, Oneness, and the Great I Am.

This is the path laid out before you. You have the freedom to choose which thought system you want to experience in any given moment. Neither thought system is better or worse than the other. Neither thought system changes Who You *are*. Both thought systems are Divine Expressions of God, but only one has the power to give you the experience of Peace, Love, and Joy in this moment. Only one has the power to restore your awareness to the Truth of Who You *are*—right now. The more consistently you choose the thought system of the Holy Spirit, the sooner you will know the awareness of God as your own.

One final note: The ego would love for you to believe that you are unworthy of enlightenment, hearing God's Voice in the world is too grand for you to pursue, you don't have enough time in your life to practice the 5 Steps, or experiencing your Oneness with God will take eons to accomplish. Remember, those are just "thoughts." They don't need to be your reality. After only a few years of immersing myself in the 5 Steps, all sense of separation is dissolving within me. I now see the Presence of God wherever I look—in everything, as everything, in both the ego and the Holy Spirit. I now experience the Presence of God in every thought I think, every emotion I feel, and everything I do, regardless of which thought system I'm experiencing. My sense of connection and Oneness is ever present in ALL that I experience.

One might think that I no longer perceive thoughts of the ego, but that is not the case. I no longer see the ego as something to solve, fix, or overcome. I see it as a divine expression of God, a divine thought that attempts to give Me *as God* the experience of what I am not—that is all. I marvel at and feel as much Love toward the experience of sadness and anger as I do toward a hug with my daughter. The illusion of separation no longer exists. It was just a temporary thought within the mind whose purpose has come to an end.

I am not special in any way to have this experience. Countless people before me have experienced the same and more. Countless people after me will do the same. I was not born with any unique abilities or advantages. I am no more capable of having this experience than you or anyone else. I simply had a deep desire within me to learn how to restore myself to Love, and I practiced the 5 Steps consistently to get myself there. We are no different from one another. You have the same desire within you to restore yourself to an ongoing experience of Love, and you have the same 5 Steps at your disposal. All you need to do now is practice them consistently. The more you practice them, the more deeply you will experience the Truth of Who You *Are*. As an Infinite Being, there is no end to the depth you can go. There is no end to the depth of the Divine Love, Truth, and Wisdom within you.

EXERCISE:
Experiencing Your True Self

To support you in experiencing your True Self, I'd like to walk you through the following meditation. Please set aside some quiet, uninterrupted time to practice this so you get as much as you can out of it.

Find a comfortable place to sit and close your eyes. Begin this meditation with **Step 1: Extend Love to Your Thoughts** and **Step 2: Feel God's Voice.**

Once you are feeling God's Presence within you as a result of **Step 2: Feel God's Voice**, with your eyes still closed I'd like you to feel your physical body. Become aware of and feel the actual sensations of your physical body. It may be the physical sensations of individual body parts or the physical sensations of your body as a whole. Once you are feeling those sensations, feel God's Presence within those sensations. Find where God's Presence exists within those physical sensations of your body. Feel into those sensations until you are able to identify God's loving Presence within them. Once you have identified God's loving Presence within the physical sensations of your body, allow yourself to just sit and be with that experience for a little while until you are ready to go to the next step.

When you are ready, while still feeling God's Presence within you, visualize your surroundings in your imagination, i.e. the room you're sitting in, your home, perhaps the street that you're living on or the surrounding area where you are meditating, etc. You can even visualize as far as the horizon. Just visualize everything that appears to be "outside" of your body. Once you see those surroundings in your imagination, allow yourself to feel God's Presence within all that you are visualizing. Allow yourself to feel God's Presence in the room or location that you're sitting in. Allow yourself to feel God's Presence in the areas surrounding your home or location. Allow yourself to feel God's Presence all around you as far as the eye can see. Stay with this meditation as long as it takes for you to identify and feel God's Presence in everything around you. Once you have felt God's Presence within everything around you, be with that experience for a while. Then allow yourself to go back and forth between feeling God's Presence within the physical sensations of your body and feeling God's Presence within your physical surroundings. Go back and forth between those two distinctions until you simultaneously feel God's Presence within your body and within your surroundings. When you are feeling God's Presence within all of it, go to the next step.

Now that you are simultaneously feeling God's Presence within the sensations of your body and within your surroundings, allow yourself to become aware of all of the sounds in your physical environment. It could be cars driving by, birds chirping, the air-conditioning whirling, or any other sounds that you hear. Feel into the sounds themselves and allow yourself to feel God's Presence within them. Feel into every sound that you hear until you are able to identify the feeling of God's Presence within them. Once you have identified God's Presence within all that you hear, allow yourself to return to feeling God's Presence within the physical sensations of your body and within all that you visualize in your surroundings. Finally, allow the feeling of God's Presence to merge between all three: your physical body, your surroundings, and all that you hear around you. Once you are feeling God's Presence within all three, proceed to the next step.

Now that you are feeling God's Presence within all that you feel, see, and hear, allow yourself to bask in God's unconditionally loving Presence for a little while. As you continue to feel that infinite Presence of God all around you and within you, when you're ready, substitute the word "Me" for the word "God" while you're feeling that all-encompassing Presence. Continue to feel that Presence and within your own mind label that Presence "Me." Feel your True Self. Feel that infinite, all expansive nature of your True Identity. Acknowledge within yourself that this is Who and What you *are*. Allow this infinite, loving Presence to be your Self and then sit with that experience for a while. Own that experience for yourself. Then when you're ready, go back to labeling that Presence "God." Label it God in your mind and then continue to feel God's loving Presence within all of creation. Then, when you're ready, go back to feeling that infinite Presence as your "Self." Spend some time feeling that Presence of God *as your Self*, using the word "Me" for your Self. Finally, go back and forth between the words "God" and "Me" until you can no longer tell the difference between them.

Once you can no longer tell the difference between your experience of God and your experience of Self, allow yourself to bask in that recognition for a little while. Take it in and enjoy it. When you're ready, open your eyes and continue to feel that infinite Presence that You as God are. Continue to feel your Self as God within all that you see, within all that you perceive and experience.

In this state of Unified Consciousness, your awareness has been restored to your True Essence, to the *Beingness* that you share with All That Is. You have pulled your identity out of the individual thoughts and things of the world and have transitioned your identity to your True Self, which is infinite, ever present, all-encompassing, and the Source of All That Is.

In Truth, there is no end to the depth that you can go within your Self. There is no end to the depth of your Beingness. Each time you practice this exercise, you will continue to go deeper and deeper into the Oneness that you share with All That Is. You will continue to go deeper and deeper into the depths of your God Consciousness, slowly but surely transforming your sense of Identity and Self away from what the ego would lead you to believe and into your most expansive, eternal Self ... until eventually you can no longer identify any distinction between Who You *are* and What God *is*.

Below is a brief recap of the steps in this meditation exercise:

1. Step 1: Extend Love to Your Thoughts.
2. Step 2: Feel God's Voice.
3. Feel the Presence of God within your physical body.
4. Feel the Presence of God within your physical surroundings.
5. Feel the Presence of God within the sounds that you hear.
6. Feel the presence of God within everything you perceive.
7. While feeling God's Presence within all things, substitute the word "Me" for "God."
8. Go back and forth between the words "Me" and "God" until you can no longer identify a difference between the two experiences.
9. Bask in the experience of your infinite, eternal Self.
10. Open your eyes and acknowledge your Divine Self in All That Is.

The Importance of Using God's Voice in the World

When one identifies with and believes the thoughts of the ego, having a framework or system in place to undo those thoughts is critical and necessary. Understanding the True Nature of God, knowing which thought system you are perceiving with in any given moment, and having access to your own Internal Guide and Teacher all work hand-in-hand as one system to migrate your awareness and identity away from the ego's thought system and to your Right-Mind so you can erase the illusion of separation and experience the Truth of Who You *Are*.

In order to accomplish that, **you must place all responsibility for the world you see into your own hands. When you are 100 percent responsible for all that you perceive and experience in the world, you give yourself 100 percent of the power to see things differently.** When you momentarily forget that your experience is the result of the way you are relating to your thoughts, you give your power away to the ego. By extending Love to your thoughts and choosing to see the world through the eyes of Holy Spirit, you reclaim that power, drain all life out of the thought system of the ego, and restore your awareness to the One Power that truly is—You.

As long as you identify with and believe the thoughts of the ego, it's absolutely essential for you to continue to seek and use God's Voice within you. Every time you become aware that you are thinking with the ego, you have the opportunity to extend Love. Every time you feel sad, angry, or fearful, you have the opportunity to embrace your emotions. Every time you are uncertain or need a friend, you have the opportunity to go within and seek communication and reassurance from this Guide and Comforter within you. You gave this Internal Teacher to your Self from the deepest part of your Being. **Allow the Holy Spirit to serve**

you until every part of your Being is restored to the awareness of its Oneness with You.

All Forms of Hearing Are Equal

Even though one is able to receive specific and clear communication from God's Voice within them by giving their Right-Mind a way to manifest words in the world, there still seems to be a drive within most people to hear God's Voice as something distinctly separate or different than their own voice. When one identifies with and believes they are the thoughts of the ego, being able to point to God's Voice, or to God's messages to you, and believe that it is not "you" or "your voice" you are listening to can be a very comforting thought.

Why is it that some people hear God's Voice within them as a seemingly separate or distinct Inner Voice, while others must give God's Voice expression through their writing or speaking in order to hear that Voice for themselves?

In the end, it all boils down to what is in your highest good in this moment, where you currently are on your path, and what your chosen purpose and unique expression of God are—right now. Neither form of hearing is better than the other. For some, hearing a specific voice within them may be just what they need to get their attention, learn the differences between the ego's voice and the Voice for Love, deliver specific messages to themselves and others, or develop the confidence they need to pursue and follow the Holy Spirit's way of thinking in their lives. For others, learning to recognize, identify with, and embody God's Voice as their own voice may be just what they need to deepen their experience of Oneness, Freedom, Responsibility, or Power in their lives.

Wanting to hear a seemingly separate or distinct Inner Voice can cause a lot of confusion and frustration for people. Know in your heart that the way you hear God's Voice is precisely what you personally need to deepen your experience of the Truth of Who You *Are* and to fulfill your unique purpose in the world. Give yourself the gift of appreciating how and why you hear God's Voice in the ways that you do. If any thoughts of the ego try to convince you that the way you hear God's Voice is not good enough, that you should be hearing differently, that you need to hear a loud voice in your head in order to trust what you hear, or that someone else hears better than you, **extend Love to those thoughts.** Give yourself the gift of remembering that you *are* God, hearing and expressing your True Self in all the ways that are in your highest good, and that there is nothing you need to do to become more than you already *are*.

Being and Creation

Being and Creation are ever present. They do not exist apart from one another. As God, you are always *being* and you are always creating in every moment.

Being is the Essence of God. It is changeless, infinite, and absolute. It is the Light that encompasses all of Creation. It is the very fabric of all thought and form. *Being* is Who and What you truly *are* and the Consciousness with which you experience all of life.

Creation, on the other hand, is the infinite expression of Being. It is the unlimited extension of God's Love through both the Holy Spirit and the ego. Creation is the mechanism through which God experiences Itself. It's the means by which God is becoming Self-Aware.

What does this mean? How does this impact your life?

No matter what you do or don't do, change or don't change, impact or don't impact in the world, you cannot alter Who and What you *are* or Who and What another *is*. You simply *are*. God simply *is*. No matter which thoughts and forms seem to rise and fall away within this vast matrix of Light, your Being (which *is* the Light itself) remains eternal and changeless. You cannot change your True Self. **No matter how hard you try, you cannot change the Reality of your Beingness. All that you can change is your awareness and expression of it.**

As the Presence of God, you have Absolute Power to express your Self in any way you desire. You can express the thought system of the ego in an unlimited number of ways, and you can express the thought system of the Holy Spirit in an unlimited number of ways. Both are equal expressions of God. The only difference between them is that one will give you an experience of what you are not, while the other will give you an experience of Who you truly *are*. One expression will be filled with the experience of fear, separation, and struggle. The other expression will be filled with the experience of Peace, Love, and Fulfillment. Both expressions *are* the Presence of Love, since all things simply *are*, but only one expression will allow you to *experience* the Love that it *is* and You *are*.

You are a creative being. You have the Freedom and Power of God to create anything you want in the world through your thinking. You are the only one who sets the rules, boundaries, and limitations in your life. You can dream, plan, pursue, and manifest whatever you want with the ego, or you can dream, plan, pursue, and manifest whatever you want with your Right-Mind. You bring the Power of God that you *are* to both ways of thinking. The question is, "Which thought system do you want to create your life with?"

Serving the One
that You Are

Many years ago, just a few months before I started hearing God's Voice within me in a clear and recognizable way, Candace and I were sitting up in bed one Sunday morning having "church" together. As usual, I was asking lots of questions and she was speaking Holy Spirit's replies out loud. One of the messages we were given that morning touched my heart deeply and planted a seed that continues to inspire and shape my heart's desire to this day. Before moving on to our next two exercises on "Discovering Your Purpose in the World" and "Connecting With Your Heart's Desire," I would like to share this message with you.

Below is an excerpt of the message from our book, *The Voice for Love: Accessing Your Inner Voice to Fulfill Your Life's Purpose*. About twenty percent of *The Voice for Love* shares our personal experiences of learning to hear and use God's Voice in our lives. The remaining eighty percent shares many of the messages and teachings we have received from Holy Spirit over the years. This message is called, *God's Puzzle*. May it touch your heart as it did mine.

NOVEMBER 18, 1999

"It is not life experience that teaches a baby to laugh. She is born with a spark of God, and that part of her remains intact. She is whole in her totality, though God is incomplete without her. This is why each one of His children (sparks of Himself) must return to Him eventually to complete the Giant Puzzle that is Source, and in doing so, each piece will finally feel its completeness. What a happy day that will be. And yet, through the perceptions in one's mind, it would be possible to experience this completeness as having already happened because, in

Truth, it has.

"If each of God's children must return to Him to complete the Puzzle, is it not true that you are a piece of that Puzzle? Is it not also true then that you have a vested interest in that Puzzle being completed? Does it do you any good to hurry back to Source when nothing can be accomplished until all of the pieces are in place? Is it true then that what would do you the most good would be to help the most amount of God's children return Home? This is the way to live.

"If what benefits the whole ultimately benefits you, then serve the whole. And do it lovingly and humbly, knowing that you are only really serving yourself. You are not doing anyone else any favors in Truth. Your call to service, then, is to serve yourself and you do this best by helping everyone along the way get to the same destination with as much Grace and dignity as possible. Can you do this? Are you doing this? How can you do this better?

"Is it not essential then to slow down and see where you could serve yourself at every opportunity? Slow down so that you can notice when you are being called to service. Service can be as small as a smile or as big as a loving thought. It only matters that you are able to be of service to those who are trying to get Home, and that you know you are doing it for yourself rather than for the other person so that there are no debts incurred in the process. How can you do this better? Be aware of this question, asking yourself continually, how can I do this better?"

Being the Voice of God in the World

There is no distinction between what you desire in your heart and what God wills for you. I'm not talking about the desires of the ego. I'm talking about the desires of your Being, the desires that originate from the Source of Love within you.

Because you and God are One, your heart's desire and your true purpose in the world are one and the same. The intentions, goals, dreams, inspirations, and passion that you discover, receive, feel, and experience in your Right-Mind are indeed the will of God being communicated to you. They are what you *as God* desire to express in the world.

As your experience of Oneness with God continues to evolve and deepen, there may be times when you experience your heart's desire and God's will for you differently. Depending upon your life experience, where you are on your spiritual path, and what it is you are learning about and strengthening in your life, there may be times when you feel drawn to know and understand your purpose in the world and how to fulfill it, and there may be times when you feel drawn to connect with and follow your heart's desire. You may even bounce back and forth between these two perspectives depending upon your mood or the challenges you're facing. It doesn't matter which perspective you choose. They will each guide you to a deeper experience of connection, fulfillment, and Oneness in your life.

To provide you with an ongoing method for fulfilling both your heart's desire and true purpose in the world, the following set of exercises is provided in duplicate. The first set focuses on discovering and fulfilling your true purpose, while the second set focuses on connecting with and following your heart's desire. In Truth, they are the same. The only difference between them is vocabulary and perspective. Practice each set of exercises for one week and then compare your experiences of each at the end.

EXERCISE
Discovering Your Purpose in the World

To feel guided, peaceful, and on-purpose in all that you do, follow the **5 Steps to Hearing God's Voice** below. Write your answer for Step 3 below and answer the questions that follow.

Step 1: Extend Love To Your Thoughts.

Step 2: Feel God's Voice.

Step 3: Ask the question, "What is my purpose in the world?"

Step 4: Express God's Voice.

Step 5: Embody God's Voice.

Question: What is my purpose in the world?

Answer:

_____

_____

_____

_____

_____

_____

_____

_____

_____

_____

_____

STEP 5: EMBODY GOD'S VOICE

Part 1. Allow yourself to fully receive the purpose that was given to you. Feel it. Be with it. Allow it to fill your heart and mind. How has your experience shifted or changed as a result of knowing your purpose? Please describe.

_____

_____

_____

_____

_____

_____

_____

_____

_____

_____

_____

_____

_____

_____

_____

_____

_____

_____

_____

_____

Part 2. Take a moment to validate that you just received communication from God about your life's purpose. How do you feel?

_____

_____

_____

_____

_____

_____

_____

_____

_____

_____

_____

_____

_____

_____

_____

_____

_____

_____

_____

_____

_____

Part 3. Spend some time extending Love to every thought and emotion that arises within you that tries to belittle, dismiss, or take away your experience of hearing God's Voice and knowing your purpose. How does extending Love to these thoughts change your experience of what you just did and the communication you received?

_____

_____

_____

_____

_____

_____

_____

_____

_____

_____

_____

_____

_____

_____

_____

_____

_____

_____

_____

EXERCISE
Fulfilling Your Purpose in the World

Once you know your purpose, your next step is to discover how you and God together want to fulfill that purpose each and every day. This daily practice will become your unique expression of God in the world. How will you express and share God's Love in the world today? Knowing this will give you the opportunity to fulfill your life's purpose every day. It will give you the inspiration, direction, and guidance you need to consciously BE the Voice of God in the world.

Each morning for the next seven days, follow the six steps below to fulfill your purpose in the world. In addition, read through the exercise on the next page entitled, **Staying in Your Right-Mind,** and incorporate those important steps throughout your day. Spend a few minutes each night journaling about your experience beginning on page 171.

Step 1: Extend Love To Your Thoughts.

Step 2: Feel God's Voice.

Step 3: Ask one of the following questions, or any derivation that works best for you, "God, what shall we do together today? What one thing can we do together today to fulfill my life's purpose? What is in the highest good for us to do together today? Where would be in the highest good for me to focus my time and energy today? What steps can I take today to fulfill my life's purpose? What would bring me true joy and peace today? What would bring me a deep sense of fulfillment today?"

Step 4: Express God's Voice.

Step 5: Embody God's Voice.

Step 6: Take action! Follow through with the inspiration and guidance you received to the best of your ability.

Staying in Your Right-Mind

Once you know your purpose and how you and God together want to express or fulfill that purpose in the world, **it's essential to be mindful of any fear, unworthiness, attachment, or any other thoughts of the ego that rise up within you AS you pursue your purpose and follow the guidance and insight you receive.** Knowing and pursuing your purpose are important, but in order to stay in your Right-Mind along the way, it is necessary to continue to acknowledge and embrace any thoughts of the ego that arise within you.

Knowing and pursuing your purpose are only a beginning. Even if you follow your heart and do exactly what you are guided to do, you will feel little fulfillment or joy in what you accomplish UNLESS you take the time to work through the fears, issues, judgments, and egoic thoughts that arise within you **along the way.** As soon as you stop embracing all of the thoughts of the ego that arise within you while you're following the guidance and inspiration you receive, you will eventually start to believe, identify with, and become those thoughts and fears of the ego. As soon as you do, you will stop experiencing the peace, joy, fulfillment, and connection you once felt in pursuing your purpose in the first place. You might take all of the right steps towards manifesting your purpose, but if you don't consciously embrace all of the egoic thoughts that arise within you along the way, your mind will be filled with fear instead of peace, striving instead of joy, and control instead of faith. You will become a human doing, not a human being. While you may physically manifest what you and God set out to share in the world, the joy of its expression will be lost to you, as well as thoroughly missed out upon along the way. By continuing to use the 5 Steps to restore yourself to your Right-Mind *as you are expressing your purpose in the world,* when a thought of the ego attempts to sweep you off your feet, you have the wherewithal to maintain your experience of peace, joy, fulfillment, gratitude, patience, certainty, connection and faith throughout your journey.

Make a commitment to yourself right now to have it all—the destination AND the journey. Discover your life's purpose and the unique expression of God you have chosen to be in the world. Seek inspiration and guidance every day about how you and God want to fulfill that purpose and expression. Then lovingly acknowledge and embrace the thoughts and emotions that arise within you along the way that attempt to take your peace, joy, and faith away from you. Doing so will unite your destination and your journey, empowering you to truly BE the Voice of God in the world. Make a commitment to restore yourself to peace, faith, gratitude, patience, and joy **along the way**, and you will surely accomplish your purpose in the world.

Follow these steps to stay in your Right-Mind throughout your day.

1. Be mindful of your experience as you pursue and fulfill your purpose. Notice any thoughts of fear, uncertainty, worry, stress, fatigue, anxiety, unworthiness, doubt, guilt, judgment, attachment, or any other thoughts of the ego that arise within you as you go about your day. Make a commitment to become aware of these thoughts.

2. Once you become aware of these thoughts and feelings, take some time to extend Love to them. You can do this the instant you notice them, or you can sit down for a few minutes at some point during your day to feel, embrace, and extend Love to those thoughts and feelings. You can also incorporate this into your regular meditation practice in order to "wipe your slate clean" before you begin your day or before you begin a specific project or activity during your day.

3. If you want, go through all **5 Steps to Hearing God's Voice**

and seek guidance and communication about any thoughts and feelings you experience.

4. Repeat these steps as often as necessary to feel guided, peaceful, and on-purpose in all that you do.

EXERCISE
Fulfilling Your Purpose Journal

The purpose of this section is to help you clarify, express, and learn from your daily experiences of fulfilling your life's purpose. Take time each evening to journal about your experiences during your day. Here are a few questions you may want to answer: What did God and I decide to express together today? Where did I follow through or not follow through with the inspiration I received? What empowered me to follow through or stopped me from following through with the guidance I received? When did I remember or forget to restore myself to my Right-Mind throughout the day? How did it feel to be "on purpose" or "not on-purpose" today?

Reflecting on your daily experiences with love, honesty, humility, understanding, and compassion is an important part of your learning and growth. Validate yourself for all the wonderful things you experienced and expressed today. If you notice any self-judgement, extend Love, Compassion, and Understanding to those thoughts and to yourself. Use this time to connect with God, not as an opportunity to beat yourself up. Be kind and gentle with yourself. Only love heals. Extend it generously to yourself during this time of reflection.

DAY 1

DAY 2

DAY 3

DAY 4

_____

_____

_____

_____

_____

_____

_____

_____

_____

_____

_____

_____

_____

_____

_____

_____

_____

_____

_____

_____

_____

_____

_____

_____

_____

_____

_____

_____

_____

_____

DAY 5

DAY 6

DAY 7

Your Heart's Desire

Every thought, expression, intention, desire, and dream within you that deepens your experience of God comes from the Holy Spirit. Because your heart's desires encompass all that brings you peace, love, joy, excitement, happiness, fulfillment, wholeness, unity, laughter, and all the other qualities of God, your heart's desires are divine expressions of God's Will for you.

Why is it difficult for many to believe in the divinity and worthiness of their heart's desires?

When one has a history of believing, identifying with, and pursuing the wants and needs of the ego, they come to learn that pursuing "their wants and needs" does not give them the peace, joy, fulfillment, and connection they truly long for. In following the desires of the ego, one is left feeling disconnected, unsatisfied, regretful, frustrated, disappointed, or one of the many other qualities of the ego. Accustomed to pursuing the false strategies and illusory rewards the ego dangles before them, it's no wonder one would doubt or avoid the desires of their heart when they they don't know the differences between the desires of their heart and those of the ego.

How can you know whether you are following the desires of the ego or those of your heart?

Apply the same litmus test discussed on pages 80-81. Take as much time as you need to feel your desires as deeply as possible. Sit with them. Be with them. Become one with them. Embrace them with all of your heart. When you do, you will discover their source.

If you experience that a particular desire is coming from a place of fear, judgment, lack, frustration, hurt, revenge, or any other thought of the ego, you can trust that the desire is not coming from your heart. If you feel into a particular desire and it brings you a deep sense of joy, connection, fulfillment, passion, wholeness, and a deeper experience of

God, you can trust that it is indeed a divine expression of God's Love.

When you discover that a particular desire is motivated by an egoic agenda, allow yourself to feel the feelings and motivations beneath that desire. Once you feel them, allow yourself to create a holy relationship with them. As you extend Love to them, the ego's thoughts and desires will melt away and you will be left feeling connected, peaceful, and whole once again.

In that place of union with your Self and God, feel into your heart and ask Holy Spirit to help reveal your heart's desires to you. When you connect with your heart's desires and feel into them more and more deeply, they will expand and grow as divine and infinite expressions of your Being. In that place of wholeness and union, you will not feel attached to your heart's desires, identified with them, or feel as if they are something you must express or fulfill in order for you or someone else to become whole or complete. You will simply experience them as loving and fulfilling expressions of your existing wholeness and Oneness with God. You will simply feel inspired to extend and share What you already *are* with the rest of your Self. You will not feel compelled to do so from a place of lack or separation. You will simply want to share your love with those who want to receive it, because that's what's in your heart to do.

EXERCISE
Connecting With Your Heart's Desire

To feel connected, passionate, and fulfilled in all that you do, follow the **5 Steps to Hearing God's Voice** below. Write your answer for Step 3 on the next page and answer the questions that follow.

Step 1: Extend Love To Your Thoughts.

Step 2: Feel God's Voice *as* your heart's desire.

Step 3: Ask the question, "What is my heart's desire?"

Step 4: Express your Self on paper or out loud to clarify and articulate your heart's desire.

Step 5: Embody God's Voice.

Question: What is my heart's desire in the world?

Answer:

STEP 5: EMBODY GOD'S VOICE

Part 1. Allow yourself to fully receive your heart's desire. Feel it. Be with it. Allow it to fill your heart and mind. How has your experience shifted or changed as a result of experiencing your heart's desire? Please describe.

_____

_____

_____

_____

_____

_____

_____

_____

_____

_____

_____

_____

_____

_____

_____

_____

_____

_____

_____

_____

_____

Part 2. Take a moment to validate that you just connected with your True Self. How do you feel?

_____

_____

_____

_____

_____

_____

_____

_____

_____

_____

_____

_____

_____

_____

_____

_____

_____

_____

_____

_____

_____

_____

Part 3. Spend some time extending Love to every thought and emotion that arises within you that tries to belittle, dismiss, or take away your experience of connecting with your True Self or discovering your heart's desire on any level. How does extending Love to these thoughts change your experience of what you just did and the insight you received?

_____

_____

_____

_____

_____

_____

_____

_____

_____

_____

_____

_____

_____

_____

_____

_____

_____

Fulfilling Your Heart's Desire

You, as an extension of love, have no other option than to extend What you *are*. When you are filled with love, you have to share it. When you are joined with the infinite Love that God is, you have to give it away. That's what love does. It extends.

The ego identifies with the forms of the world and attempts to manipulate them in order to meet its needs for survival. The ego pursues its desires in the world because it sees itself and the world as separate, incomplete, lacking, broken, unhealed, unholy, and in need of repair. The Holy Spirit, on the other hand, extends love in the world from a place of wholeness, completion, and unity. The Holy Spirit looks beyond all forms to the infinite and perfect wholeness of Spirit that You, as God, truly *are*.

Your heart's desires are given to you as divine expressions of the Holy Spirit's vision. They are given to you to express, share, and enjoy from a place of wholeness and completion. You do not need to fulfill your heart's desires in order to save or fix yourself or the world. Seen through God's eyes, you are not broken. You are whole and complete, just as your brothers and sisters are. There is nothing that needs to be accomplished in the world of form in order for this to be true. You remain as God created you to be.

This does not mean, however, that you should do nothing or take no action in the world. Far from it. It simply means that when you're joined with the Holy Spirit, you are free to extend and express your love in the world from a place of wholeness and completion without the ego's agendas or beliefs in separation.

There is a call deep within you to extend your love in the world. It is this call within you that motivates you to extend Love to all that arises in your awareness. If every thought of the ego is indeed a "call for love," it is your heart's desire to learn how to consistently respond to that call with love.

Your brothers and sisters in the world are the same as you. Even though they are whole and complete in God's eyes, they do not always experience that Truth for themselves. They are in the habit of believing and identifying with the thoughts of the ego. Because you and your brothers and sisters share one heart and mind with God, every call for love in the world is truly your own call for love. It does not matter whether the call appears to come from within you or "out there" in the world. It is the same call. This is why your heart's desire to extend Love within you is the same as your heart's desire to extend Love to all that appears to be "out there in the world."

It is your heart's desire to join with every part of yourself in celebration, joy, happiness, and union. It is your heart's desire to join with every part of your Self that is not fully aware of its union with you. **Allow yourself to BE the divine Presence of God's Love in expression in the world.** Join with, embrace, and extend Love to all that arises within you and to all that arises in the world.

When one is identified with the ego, he or she would say, "Of myself I do nothing, but through me all things will be done."

When one is identified *as* the Presence of God in the world, he or she would say, "Of the ego I do nothing, but through my expression in the world, I will do all things."

You *are* the Presence of God in the world. Know the Truth of Who you are. Allow yourself to embrace the desires of your heart *as* God's Will and Expression. Pursue your heart's desires out of love and joy. Every moment you do, you extend God's Love as your own.

EXERCISE
Staying in Your Right-Mind

As you begin to express your heart's desires in the world, it's important to be mindful of any fears, unworthiness, personal agendas, attachments, or any other thoughts of the ego that arise within you. This is a critical step in removing the poison from your passion. Knowing and pursuing your heart's desires is wonderful, but **in order to stay in your Right-Mind along the way,** it is necessary to continue to acknowledge and embrace the thoughts of the ego as they arise.

As God, you can express anything you truly desire through your heart and mind. By being in your Right-Mind (Step 1), feeling your connection (Step 2), and seeking inspiration and guidance (Steps 3-4), you can become absolutely certain of your heart's desires and know how you want to express them. These are not steps you take just once. These are steps you take repeatedly, over and over and over again. When you continue to use the 5-Steps to restore yourself to your Right-Mind **along the way,** when a thought of the ego arises within you while you're pursuing your heart's desires, you have the wherewithal to maintain your experience of peace, joy, passion, fulfillment, wholeness, gratitude, patience, clarity, certainty, integrity, kindness, generosity, connection, and faith **throughout your journey.** That is a huge gift.

Don't be content to merely discover and manifest your heart's desires in the world. The outcome is not more important than the journey. What you manifest is not more important than your state of mind or experience along the way. **Make a commitment to yourself to have it all—the destination AND the journey.** Discover your heart's desires and the unique expressions of God you desire to *be* in the world. Seek inspiration and guidance every day about how you want to fulfill those desires. Then lovingly acknowledge and embrace the thoughts and emotions of the ego that arise within you *throughout your journey* which attempt to take your peace, joy, love, and faith from you.

"The 5 Steps" are an iterative process. They not only help you to connect with your Self and begin your journey with gratitude, confidence, faith, enthusiasm, passion, and certainty, they also help you to maintain your integrity throughout your journey as well. By continuing to extend Love to all that arises within you and by continuing to seek connection, guidance, and inspiration along the way, you empower yourself to truly BE the Voice of God in the world. Make a commitment—RIGHT NOW—to restore yourself to peace, faith, gratitude, patience, and joy *along the way*, and you will surely fulfill your heart's desires in the world.

1. Be mindful of your inner experience as you take steps to fulfill your heart's desires. Notice any thoughts of fear, uncertainty, worry, stress, fatigue, anxiety, unworthiness, doubt, guilt, judgment, attachment, or any other thoughts of the ego that arise within you as you go about your day. Make a commitment to become aware of these thoughts.

2. Once you become aware of these thoughts and feelings, take some time to extend Love to them. You can do this the instant you notice them, or you can sit down for a few minutes during your day to feel, embrace, and extend Love to them. You can also incorporate this step into your regular meditation practice in order to "wipe your slate clean" before you begin your day or before you begin a specific project or activity during your day.

3. If you want, go through all **5 Steps to Hearing God's Voice** and seek guidance and communication about any thoughts and feelings you experience.

4. Repeat these steps as often as necessary to feel connected, passionate, and fulfilled in all that you do.

EXERCISE
Fulfilling Your Heart's Desire Journal

The purpose of this section is to help you clarify, express, and learn from fulfilling your heart's desires on a daily basis. Take time each evening to journal about your experiences during the day. Here are a few questions you may want to answer: What were my heart's desires to express today? Where did I follow through or not follow through with my heart's desires? What empowered me to follow through or stopped me from following through with my heart's desires? When did I remember or forget to restore myself to my Right-Mind throughout the day? How did it feel to express my heart's desires today?

Reflecting on your daily experiences with love, honesty, humility, understanding, and compassion is an important part of your learning and growth. Validate yourself for all the wonderful things you experienced and expressed today. If you notice any self-judgment, extend Love, Compassion, and Understanding to those thoughts and to yourself. Use this time to connect with yourself, not as an opportunity to beat yourself up. Be kind and gentle with yourself. Only love heals. Extend it generously to yourself during this time of reflection.

DAY 1

_____

_____

_____

_____

_____

_____

_____

_____

_____

_____

_____

_____

_____

_____

_____

_____

_____

_____

_____

_____

_____

_____

_____

_____

_____

_____

DAY 2

DAY 3

DAY 4

_____

_____

_____

_____

_____

_____

_____

_____

_____

_____

_____

_____

_____

_____

_____

_____

_____

_____

_____

_____

DAY 5

DAY 6

DAY 7

EXERCISE
Comparing Your Experiences

1. How was your experience of fulfilling your life's purpose on a daily basis SIMILAR to your experience of fulfilling your heart's desires on a daily basis? Please describe.

_____

_____

_____

_____

_____

_____

_____

_____

_____

_____

_____

_____

_____

_____

_____

_____

_____

_____

2. How was your experience of fulfilling your life's purpose on a daily basis DIFFERENT from your experience of fulfilling your heart's desires on a daily basis? Please describe.

_____

_____

_____

_____

_____

_____

_____

_____

_____

_____

_____

_____

_____

_____

_____

_____

_____

_____

_____

_____

3. Did one perspective feel more comfortable, fulfilling, or enjoyable than the other? If so, why do you think that was? Please describe.

4. Was one perspective easier to follow through with than the other? If so, why do you think that was? Please describe.

_____

_____

_____

_____

_____

_____

_____

_____

_____

_____

_____

_____

_____

_____

_____

_____

_____

_____

_____

_____

_____

_____

_____

_____

Love in Action

What you have learned and experienced throughout this book is just a beginning. The Truth is, there is no end. God is infinite. You are infinite. There is no end to the expansion, depth, union, love, and oneness you can experience. If there were an end, God would be finite. And that is not the case. There is no end to the extension of God's Love.

What does this mean for you?

It means that you're only touching the tip of what's possible for you to experience right here, right now, this lifetime, and beyond. Hearing God's Voice is not an end. It's a beginning. There truly is no end to this journey of awakening. We all love to imagine what it would be like to finally become "finished," to reach that end goal or "destination." But there is no such end. The most enlightened beings you know—who are truly You dressed up in different garments—are still evolving and deepening their experience of Love, Unity, and Self.

Every fragment of your One Consciousness must eventually take this journey of awakening until every tiny piece of your Self is united in the awareness of your Oneness. (The word "Self" means everyone and everything in all of creation.) This is why every awakened, self-realized "master" has but one desire—to awaken the rest of their Self. At the core of our *being,* this one desire exists within all of us: to join and serve God, to join and serve our One Self.

What is required of you to bring that about? Choice. Commitment. Practice. Consistency. Dedication. Desire. Passion. Patience. Grace. Humor. And every other expression of Love that restores your awareness to your Self in each moment.

Just because the path laid out before you has no end does not mean there is nowhere to go. Just because there is no need to rush within eternity doesn't mean you should not take action now. Just because you are already perfect in Truth doesn't mean there is no need to accomplish anything in the world.

Live your life with passion, joy, wonder, adventure, and commitment to extending your Love in all the ways of your heart. Dedicate your life to mastering the 5 Steps in every area of your life. Imagine the clarity, certainty, love, passion, creativity, and fulfillment you would feel if you were always aware of the profound Oneness and Love that you truly *are* in every moment. Imagine the impact, transformation, and healing you would inspire in others if you brought that state of awareness into all of your relationships and into everything you did.

If you are not practicing these 5 Steps on a regular basis, make a commitment to yourself—RIGHT NOW—to do so. Understanding these ideas and concepts will only take you so far. PRACTICING these steps each and every day until they become part of you will transform your life beyond what you can imagine.

You have the power of God at your disposal, and you can do anything you want with it. You can use this power to awaken your Self to the full realization of Who and What you truly *are*, or you can use this power to pretend to be who and what you are truly not.

You have the freedom to choose in every moment how you want to relate to your thoughts, your Self, and the world. You have the choice in every moment to see through the eyes of Holy Spirit and recognize the face of God before you, or to see through the eyes of ego and perceive a world of struggle, injustice, death, and despair. You have the opportunity to share love, inspiration, and truth with your brothers and sisters, or to wallow in the distractions, pain, and disempowering beliefs of the ego. This is the choice that you *as God* have in the world. You have the choice in every moment which voice you want to listen to and express, and you make this choice over and over and over again with every breath you take.

Celebrate, enjoy, and make use of the precious time you have in the world. Time, just like thought, is the opportunity to extend Love, serve your One Self, and BE the Presence of Peace and Love IN ACTION in the world.

Every moment you choose Love, Peace, Happiness, or Celebration is a moment you experience Heaven on Earth. Every moment you choose Joy, Passion, Ease, or Connection is a moment of knowing your True Freedom and Power *as God* in the world.

Embrace every moment you are given, and all that God *is* will be yours.

Thank You.

I Love You.

I am with You always.

Contact Information

DavidPaul Doyle and his wife, Candace Doyle, are the founders of The Voice for Love, a leading nonprofit organization and global community of people who join together to give and receive love, communication, inspiration, learning, and support for hearing God's Voice in their lives.

The Voice for Love's worldwide team of students and certified spiritual counselors, coaches, and teachers provides education and training through its free telephone hotline, training and resource center, and through its many public events, including workshops, weekend intensives, tele-seminars, and certification programs throughout the world.

For more information and to get involved in this growing movement of true personal empowerment, visit www.thevoiceforlove.com or contact:

The Voice for Love
P.O. Box 3125
Ashland, OR 97520
Phone: 541-488-0426
www.thevoiceforlove.com
love@thevoiceforlove.com